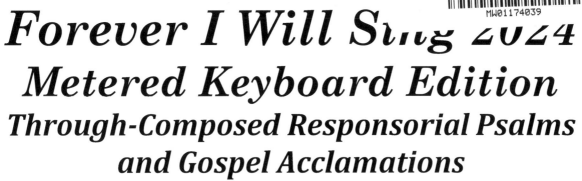

# Forever I Will Sing 2024
## Metered Keyboard Edition
### Through-Composed Responsorial Psalms and Gospel Acclamations

December 3, 2023 – November 18, 2024

Year B

Music by Timothy R. Smith

**Online Instructional Videos**
Visit www.timothyrsmith.com for links to online instructional videos for each of the Responsorial Psalms and Gospel Acclamations. These are helpful in familiarizing cantors and instrumentalists with each piece.

**Refrain Melodies for Assembly Worship Aids**
To receive pdf of all refrain melodies at no additional charge, send copy of receipt to forever@timothyrsmith.com

*Forever I Will Sing 2024 (Metered Keyboard Edition)*
Through-Composed Responsorial Psalms and Gospel Acclamations
Year B – December 3, 2023 through November 18, 2024

Musical settings by Timothy R. Smith
This songbook © 2023, Timothy R. Smith. Published by TR TUNE, LLC. All rights reserved.
www.timothyrsmith.com
ISBN: 978-1-7350150-8-8

All musical settings by Timothy R. Smith. Some settings were previously published by OCP, 5536 NE Hassalo, Portland, OR 97213-3638; as indicated, they are available at www.ocp.org

Also available at www.timothyrsmith.com:
*Forever I Will Sing 2024 Metered Guitar/Vocal Edition*
*Forever I Will Sing 2024 Classic Chant Edition*

Publisher:    TR TUNE, LLC, Waterford, MI   www.timothyrsmith.com
Composer:    Timothy R. Smith
Editor:        Barbara Bridge
Cover Art:    Mary Dudek
                www.marydudekart.com

We are still developing and refining this format and we welcome any feedback. Please feel free to contact me anytime if you have feedback about any aspect of this publication.

Tim Smith
tim@timothyrsmith.com

# Singing the Psalm Settings

**Psalm Refrains** can be adapted to piano, organ, guitar accompaniment, or even SATB choir. The melodies, rhythms and harmonies are designed to embody the spirit of the text.

**Verses** are set for solo voice (Cantor) with keyboard or guitar accompaniment. The Guitar Edition features fewer page turns for easier use. The Classic Chant Edition features non-metered verses stacked with similar melodic contours. Refrains are uniform among all editions.

**The mixed-meter settings** of many of these Psalms were developed from extensive use of *Forever I Will Sing Classic Chant Edition* (still available for 2023). In the chant settings I became more aware of the natural rhythm of text. These settings are based on my perception of those natural rhythms.

Similar to how digital code is based on a series of *ones* and *zeros*, I believe rhythm of language can be based on syllable groupings of *twos* and *threes,* or *duples* and *triples*. In Example 1 consider the text in Psalm 105: *You descendants of Abraham, his servants.* I perceive the natural rhythm as this configuration of duples and triples:

In this instance, *descendants of* is a triple rhythm and the others are all duple. (eighth note = eighth note)

Consider in Example 2 this segment of Psalm 98:

## Why not indicate the time signature changes?
While some of these Psalms fit within traditional time signatures, many of the settings in this book are driven by the duple/triple natural language rhythm. Since there is no recurring metric structure in this mixed meter environment, we feel indicating constantly changing time signatures would add unnecessary distraction. These rhythms are implemented by following the lowest value of the duple/triple rhythmic groupings – often the eighth note.

Of course, there are no absolutes. In Example 3, Psalm 116 (p. 84), the natural text rhythm inspires a specific novel rhythm in which the quarter note is the fundamental beat.

Also note the triplet rhythm (*3*) in which 3 eighth notes fill the duration of 2 eighth notes – This is the exception. Keep in mind that all eighth notes are equal (as in Examples 1 & 2), whether beamed in twos or threes *unless* there is a triplet (*3*) indicator as seen below:

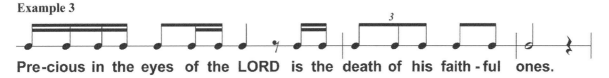

# Scriptural Index

| Page | Scripture Reference |
|------|---------------------|
| 188 | Daniel 3:52, 53, 54, 55, 56 |
| 132 | Exodus 15:1-2, 3-4, 5-6, 17-18 |
| 139 | Isaiah 12:2-3, 4bcd, 5-6 |
| 146 | Isaiah 12:2-3, 4bcd, 5-6 |
| 19 | Judith 13:18bcde, 19 |
| 22 | Luke 1:46–48, 49–50, 53–54 |
| 161 | Psalm 4:2, 4, 7–8, 9 |
| 257 | Psalm 15:2–3, 3–4, 4–5 |
| 126 | Psalm 16:5, 8, 9-10, 11 |
| 306 | Psalm 16:5, 8, 9-10, 11 |
| 298 | Psalm 18:2–3, 3–4, 47, 51 |
| 272 | Psalm 19:8, 10, 12–13, 14 |
| 84 | Psalm 19:8, 9, 10, 11 |
| 142 | Psalm 19:8, 9, 10, 11 |
| 191 | Psalm 19:8, 9, 10, 11 |
| 167 | Psalm 22:26–27, 28, 30, 31–32 |
| 106 | Psalm 22:8-9, 17-18, 19-20, 23-24 |
| 93 | Psalm 23:1-3a, 3b-4, 5, 6 |
| 232 | Psalm 23:1–3, 3–4, 5, 6 |
| 293 | Psalm 24:1bc-2, 3-4ab, 5-6 |
| 62 | Psalm 25:4–5, 6–7, 8–9 |
| 78 | Psalm 25:4–5, 6–7, 8–9 |
| 326 | Psalm 27:1, 4, 13-14 |
| 136 | Psalm 30:2, 4, 5-6, 11-12, 13 |
| 223 | Psalm 30:2, 4, 5–6, 11, 12, 13 |
| 114 | Psalm 31:2, 6, 12-13, 15-16, 17, 25 |
| 72 | Psalm 32:1–2, 5, 11 |
| 184 | Psalm 33:10-11, 12-13, 14-15 |
| 314 | Psalm 33:4-5, 12-13, 18-19, 20 & 22 |
| 124 | Psalm 33:4-5, 6-7, 12-13, 20 & 22 |
| 284 | Psalm 33:4–5, 18–19, 20, 22 |
| 203 | Psalm 33:4–5, 6, 9, 18–19, 20, 22 |
| 250 | Psalm 34:2-3, 4-5, 6-7 |
| 253 | Psalm 34:2–3, 16–17, 18–19, 20–21 |
| 240 | Psalm 34:2–3, 4–5, 6–7, 8–9 |
| 58 | Psalm 40:2, 4, 7–8, 8–9, 10 |
| 143 | Psalm 42:3, 5; 43:3, 4 |
| 248 | Psalm 45:10, 11, 12, 16 |
| 175 | Psalm 47:2-3, 6-7, 8-9 |
| 147 | Psalm 51:12-13, 14-15, 18-19 |
| 74 | Psalm 51:3-4, 5-6ab, 12-13, 14 & 17 |
| 97 | Psalm 51:3–4, 12–13, 14–15 |
| 268 | Psalm 54:3–4, 5, 6 & 8 |
| 51 | Psalm 67:2–3, 5, 6, 8 |
| 54 | Psalm 72:1–2, 7–8, 10–11, 12–13 |
| 237 | Psalm 78:3–4, 23–24, 25, 54 |

| Page | Scripture Reference |
|------|---------------------|
| 8 | Psalm 80:2–3, 15–16, 18–19 |
| 16 | Psalm 85:9–10, 11–12, 13–14 |
| 229 | Psalm 85:9–10, 11–12, 13–14 |
| 26 | Psalm 89:2-3, 4-5, 27, 29 |
| 29 | Psalm 89:4-5, 16-17, 27, 29 |
| 281 | Psalm 90:12–13, 14–15, 16–17 |
| 214 | Psalm 92:2–3, 13–14, 15–16 |
| 307 | Psalm 93:1, 1–2, 5 |
| 88 | Psalm 95:1-2, 6-7, 8-9 |
| 65 | Psalm 95:1–2, 6–7, 7–9 |
| 33 | Psalm 96:1-2, 2-3, 11-12, 13 |
| 38 | Psalm 97:1, 6, 11-12 |
| 40 | Psalm 98:1, 2-3, 3-4, 5-6 |
| 171 | Psalm 98:1, 2–3, 3–4 |
| 12 | Psalm 98:1, 2–3ab, 3cd–4 |
| 179 | Psalm 103:1–2, 11–12, 19–20 |
| 322 | Psalm 103:8 & 10, 13-14, 15-16, 17-18 |
| 196 | Psalm 104:1-2, 24 & 35, 27-28, 29-30 |
| 120 | Psalm 104:1-2, 5-6, 10, 12, 13-14, 24, 35 |
| 200 | Psalm 104:1, 24, 29-30, 31, 34 |
| 44 | Psalm 105:1–2, 3–4, 5–6, 8–9 |
| 192 | Psalm 107:2-3, 4-5, 6-7, 8-9 |
| 218 | Psalm 107:23-24, 25-26, 28-29, 30-31 |
| 310 | Psalm 113:1-2, 3-4, 5-6, 7-8 |
| 264 | Psalm 116:1–2, 3–4, 5–6, 8–9 |
| 81 | Psalm 116:10, 15, 16–17, 18–19 |
| 111 | Psalm 116:12-13, 15-16bc, 17-18 |
| 208 | Psalm 116:12–13, 15–16, 17–18 |
| 150 | Psalm 118:1-2, 16-17, 22-23 |
| 153 | Psalm 118:1-2, 16-17, 22-23 |
| 164 | Psalm 118:1, 8–9, 21–23, 26, 28, 29 |
| 156 | Psalm 118:2-4, 13-15, 22-24 |
| 224 | Psalm 123:1–2, 2, 3–4 |
| 288 | Psalm 126:1–2, 2–3, 4–5, 6 |
| 319 | Psalm 128:1-2, 3, 4-5 |
| 48 | Psalm 128:1-2, 3, 4-5, 6 |
| 277 | Psalm 128:1–2, 3, 4–5, 6 |
| 102 | Psalm 130:1-2, 3-4, 5-6, 7-8 |
| 212 | Psalm 130:1-2, 3-4, 5-6, 7-8 |
| 244 | Psalm 132:6-7, 9-10, 13-14 |
| 89 | Psalm 137:1–2, 3, 4–5, 6 |
| 233 | Psalm 145:10–11, 15–16, 17–18 |
| 260 | Psalm 146:6-7, 8–9, 9–10 |
| 302 | Psalm 146:7, 8–9, 9–10 |
| 69 | Psalm 147:1–2, 3–4, 5–6 |

# Refrain Index

# First Sunday of Advent

*December 3*

Psalm 80:2-3, 15-16, 18-19

(M.M. ♩ = c. 60)

**REFRAIN**

Lord, make us turn to you; let us see your face and we shall be saved.

**Verse 1**

O shep-herd of Is-ra-el, heark-en, from your throne up-on the cher-u-bim, shine forth. Rouse your pow'r and come to save us. [Come to save us.]

*to Refrain*

Music © 1996, Timothy R. Smith. Published by OCP. All rights reserved. Through composed score available in *Blessed Assurance* songbook 10747 available at www.ocp.org.

8

*to Refrain*

**Verse 3**

May your help be with the man of your right hand, with the son of man whom

Em

you your-self made strong. Then we will no more with-draw from you; give us new

G/D    Cmaj7                    D/A        Asus2        Cmaj7

*to Refrain*

life, and we will call up-on your name.

D/A                Asus2        C        D        Em

**REFRAIN**

Em              D/E        Cmaj7/E        D/E        Am7    Bm7    Esus4

Lord, make us turn to you;    let us see your face    and    we    shall be saved.

**Note: Response reprinted for convenience.**

10

## Gospel Acclamation: cf. Psalm 85:8

**Acclamation:** (Keyboard/SATB) NO. III

Al - le - lu - ia, al - le - lu - ia.

**Verse: (Cantor)**

Show us, Lord, your love; / and grant us your sal - vation.

Music © 2014, Timothy R. Smith. Published by TR TUNE, LLC. All rights reserved.

# The Immaculate Conception of the Blessed Virgin Mary

*December 8*

**Verse 2**

The LORD has made his sal - va - tion known: in the sight of the

Am      Fmaj7      G      Em      Am      Fadd2      Gsus2
Dm      B♭maj7      C      Am      Dm      B♭add2      Csus2

na - tions he has re - vealed his jus - tice. He has re - mem - bered his

Am      Fmaj7      Gsus2      Am      Dm
Dm      B♭maj7      Csus2      Dm      Gm

*to Refrain*

kind - ness and his faith - ful - ness toward the house of Is - ra - el.____

G/B      C      Am      F      Bdm7/D      Esus4      E
C/E      F      Dm      B♭      Edm7/G      Asus4      A

**Verse 3**

*to Refrain*

**REFRAIN**

**Note: Response reprinted for convenience.**

## Gospel Acclamation: Luke 1:28

**Acclamation:** (Keyboard/SATB) NO. IV

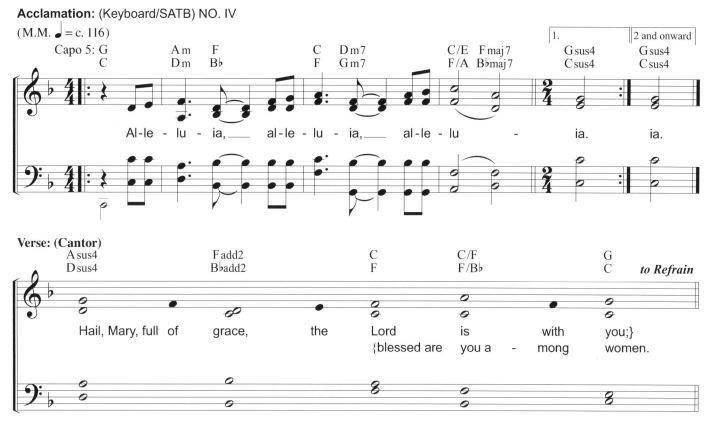

**Verse: (Cantor)**

# Second Sunday of Advent

*December 10*

Psalm 85:9, 10, 11-12, 13-14

(M.M. ♩ = c. 90)

**REFRAIN**

Lord, let us see your kind-ness, and grant us your sal - va - tion.____

**Verse 1** (M.M. ♩ = c. 76)

I will hear what God pro - claims; the__ LORD— for he pro-claims

peace to his peo - ple.__ Near in - deed is his sal - va - tion to

*to Refrain*

those who fear him, glo - ry dwell-ing in our land.

*accel.*

**Verse 2** (M.M. ♩ = c. 76)

Kind-ness and truth shall meet; jus-tice and peace shall kiss. Truth shall spring out of the

G  D A m D E m C sus2

*to Refrain*

earth, and jus-tice shall look down from __ heav-en.

D G/B G/D C/E A m/C D

*accel.*

**Verse 3** (M.M. ♩ = c. 76)

The LORD him-self will give his ben-e-fits; our __ land shall yield its

G D A m

in - crease. Jus - tice shall walk be - fore him, and pre -

E m C sus2 D

*to Refrain*

pare the way of his steps.

G/B   G/D   C/E   Am/C   D

*accel.*

**REFRAIN** (M.M. ♩ = c. 90)

Em                    G              D            C

Lord, let us see your kind-ness, and grant us your sal - va - tion.

**Note: Response reprinted for convenience.**

## Gospel Acclamation: Luke 3:4, 6

**Acclamation:** (Keyboard/SATB) NO. I

(♩ = c. 96)

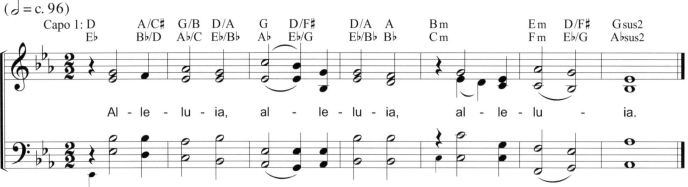

Al - le - lu - ia, al - le - lu - ia, al - le - lu - ia.

**Verse:** (Cantor)                                                                *to Refrain*

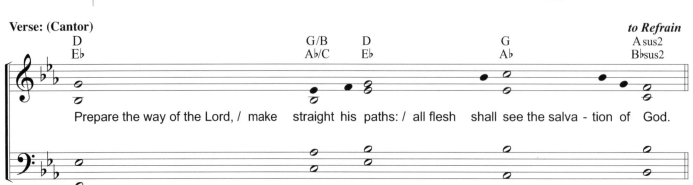

Prepare the way of the Lord, / make straight his paths: / all flesh shall see the salva - tion of God.

# Our Lady of Guadalupe

*December 12*

*"Sunday, December 12 is the Third Sunday of Advent, and the Feast of Our Lady of Guadalupe is omitted this year. Our Lady of Guadalupe may be appropriately honored in the Homily, Universal Prayer, and hymns during the Sunday liturgy. If pastoral advantage calls for it (cf. GIRM, no. 376), a Votive Mass of Our Lady of Guadalupe may be celebrated on a weekday before or after December 12, with the proper readings and prayers."*
United States Conference of Catholic Bishops Committee on Divine Worship

Judith 13:18bcde, 19

**Verse 2**

*to Refrain*

**REFRAIN**

Note: Response reprinted for convenience

## Gospel Acclamation:

**Acclamation:** (Keyboard/SATB) NO. II

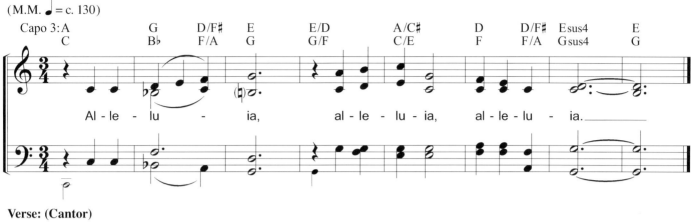

Al - le - lu - ia, al - le - lu - ia, al - le - lu - ia.

**Verse: (Cantor)**

Blessed are you, holy Vir - gin Mary, / de - serving of all praise; from

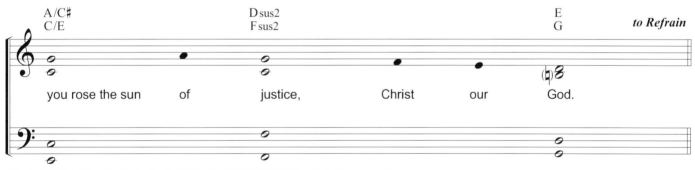

you rose the sun of justice, Christ our God.

*to Refrain*

# Third Sunday of Advent

*December 17*

Luke 1:46–48, 49–50, 53–54

www.timothyrsmith.com

**Verse 2**

The Al - might - y has done great things for me, and

A m/C   G/B   D/A

ho - ly is his Name. He has mer - cy on those who

D m/F   E m7/G   D/A   F maj7   G/B

*to Refrain*

fear him ___ in eve - ry gen - er - a - tion.

A/C♯   D m7   E m7   D m/F   G   A

**Verse 3**

He has filled the hun - gry with good things, and the rich he has

A m/C   G/B   D/A   D m/F

sent a - way emp - ty.___ He has come to the help of his ser - vant

Is - ra - el for he has re - mem - bered his prom - ise of mer - cy,___

*to Refrain*

**REFRAIN**

My soul re - joic - es in my God. My soul re - joic - es in my God.

**Note: Response reprinted for convenience.**

**Gospel Acclamation**: Isaiah 61:1 (cited in Luke 4:18)

**Acclamation:** (Keyboard/SATB) NO. IV

Al - le - lu - ia,___ al - le - lu - ia,___ al - le - lu - ia. ia.

**Verse: (Cantor)**                                                                                                *to Refrain*

The Spirit of the Lord is up - on me, / because he has a - nointed me to bring glad tidings to the poor.

# Fourth Sunday of Advent

*December 24*

*to Refrain*

kind-ness is es-tab-lished for - ev-er"; in heav-en you have con-firmed your faith-ful-ness.

A m           E m      G/F           A sus2

*accel.*

**Verse 2** (M.M. ♩ = c. 76)

"I have made a cov-e-nant with my cho-sen one, I have sworn to Da-vid my ser-vant: For-

D      A m      G sus2      C sus2    F/B♭    D sus2

*to Refrain*

ev-er will I con - firm your pos - ter-i-ty and es-tab-lish your throne for all gen-er - a-tions."

D      A m      E m           G/F      A sus2

*accel.*

**Verse 3** (M.M. ♩ = c. 76)

"He shall say of me, 'You are my fa-ther, my God, the Rock my sav - ior.' For-

D      A m      G sus2      C sus2    F/B♭    D sus2

27

*to Refrain*

ev-er I will main-tain my kind-ness toward him, and my cov-e-nant with him stands firm."

*accel.*

**REFRAIN**

For ev-er I___ will sing the good-ness of___ the Lord. For

ev - er I will sing___ the good - ness of___ the Lord.

**Note: Response reprinted for convenience**

## Gospel Acclamation: Luke 1:38

**Acclamation:** (Keyboard/SATB) NO. II

(M.M. ♩ = c. 130)

Al - le - lu - ia, al - le - lu - ia, al - le - lu - ia.___

**Verse: (Cantor)**

*to Refrain*

Behold, I am the handmaid of the Lord. / May it be done to me ac - cord-ing to your word.

# The Nativity of The Lord (Christmas): At the Vigil Mass

*December 24*

Psalm 89:4-5, 16-17, 27, 29

*to Refrain*

ter - i - ty    and    es - tab - lish your    throne    for    all    gen - er - - a - tions.

Em    G/F    Asus2

*accel.*

**Verse 2**   (M.M. ♩ = c. 76)

Bless - ed    the    peo - ple    who    know the    joy - ful    shout;    in    the    light    of    your

D    Am    Gsus2    Csus2

coun - te - nance, O    LORD; they    walk.    At    your name    they re - joice    all    the day,

F/B♭    Dsus2    D    Am    Em

*to Refrain*    **Verse 3**   (M.M. ♩ = c. 76)

and through your    jus - tice they    are    ex - alt - ed.    He    shall    say    of    me,

G/F    Asus2    D

*accel.*

30

**Note: Response reprinted for convenience**

## Gospel Acclamation:

**Acclamation:** (Keyboard/SATB) NO. V

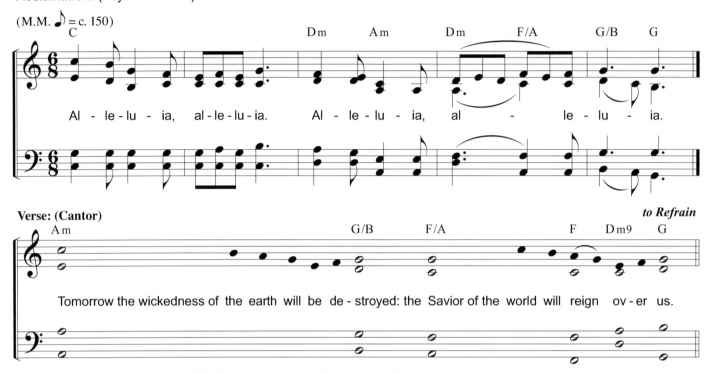

Al - le - lu - ia, al - le - lu - ia. Al - le - lu - ia, al - le - lu - ia.

**Verse: (Cantor)** *to Refrain*

Tomorrow the wickedness of the earth will be de - stroyed: the Savior of the world will reign ov - er us.

# The Nativity of the Lord (Christmas): At the Mass during the Night

*December 25*

Psalm 96:1-2, 2-3, 11-12, 13

To-day is born our Sav-ior, Christ, the Lord, Christ the Lord. To-day is born our Sav-ior, Christ the Lord.

**Verse 1**

Sing to the LORD a new song; sing to the LORD, all you lands. Sing to the LORD; bless his name.

*to Refrain*

**Verse 2**

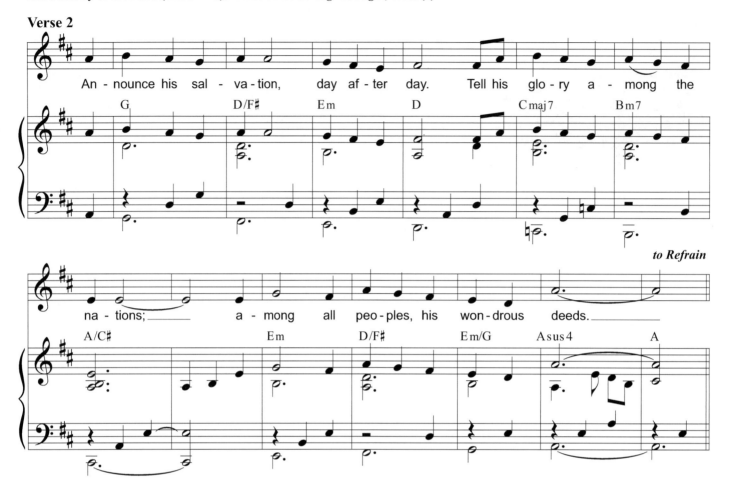

**REFRAIN**

**Note: Response reprinted for convenience**

**Verse 3**

Let the heav-ens be glad and the earth re - joice; let the sea and what

fills it re - sound;_____ let the plains be joy-ful and all that is in them!

*to Refrain*

Then shall all the trees of the for - est ex - ult._____

**Verse 4**

**REFRAIN**

Today is born our Savior, Christ, __ the Lord, Christ __ the Lord. To-

day is born our Savior, Christ the Lord. __

**Note: Response reprinted for convenience**

**Gospel Acclamation**: Luke 2:10-11

**Acclamation:** (Keyboard/SATB) NO. V

(M.M. ♩ = c. 150)

Al - le - lu - ia, al - le - lu - ia. Al - le - lu - ia, al - le - lu - ia.

**Verse: (Cantor)**                                                                                               *to Refrain*

I proclaim to you good news of great joy: / to - day a Sav - ior is born for us, Christ the Lord.

# The Nativity of the Lord (Christmas): At the Mass at Dawn

*December 25*

Psalm 97:1, 6, 11-12

**Verse 2**

**Gospel Acclamation**: Luke 2:14

**Acclamation:** (Keyboard/SATB) NO. V

# The Nativity of the Lord (Christmas): At the Mass during the Day

*December 25*

All the ends of the earth have seen the sav-ing power of God.

Sing to the LORD a new song, for he has done won-drous deeds; his

right hand has won vic-t'ry for him, his ho-ly arm.

**Verse 2** (M.M. ♩ = c. 71)

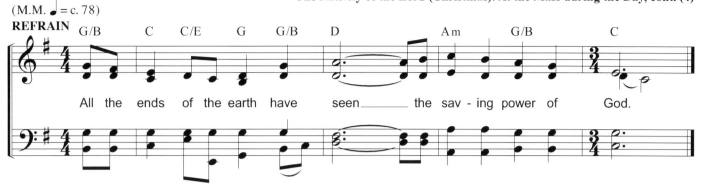

**REFRAIN**

All the ends of the earth have seen_____ the sav - ing power of God.

**Note: Response reprinted for convenience**

## Gospel Acclamation:

**Acclamation:** (Keyboard/SATB) NO. V

Al - le - lu - ia, al - le - lu - ia. Al - le - lu - ia, al - le - lu - ia.

**Verse: (Cantor)**

A hol - y day has dawned up - on us. Come, you na - tions, and a -

*to Refrain*

dore the Lord. / For to - day a great light has come up - on the earth.

# The Holy Family of Jesus, Mary and Joseph

*Optional Year B*
*December 31*

Psalm 105:1–2, 3–4, 5–6, 8–9

(M.M. ♩ = c. 66)

**REFRAIN**

The Lord re-mem-bers his cov-e-nant for ev-er.

**Verse 1**

Give thanks to the LORD, in-voke his name; make known a-mong the na-tions his deeds. Sing to him, sing his praise, pro-claim all his won-drous deeds.

*to Refrain*

**Verse 2**

Glo-ry in his ho-ly name; re-joice, O hearts that seek the LORD! Look to the

*to Refrain*

LORD in his strength; con-stant-ly seek his__ face.

**Verse 3**

You de-scend-ants of A-bra-ham, his ser-vants, sons of

Ja-cob, his cho-sen__ ones! He, the LORD, is our

*to Refrain*

God; through-out the earth his judg-ments pre-vail.

**Verse 4**

**REFRAIN**

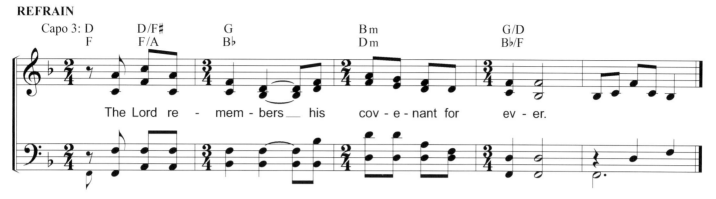

**Note: Response reprinted for convenience**

## Gospel Acclamation: Hebrew 1:1-2
**Acclamation:** (Keyboard/SATB) NO. III

(M.M. ♩ = c. 160)

**Verse: (Cantor)**                                                                                    *to Refrain*

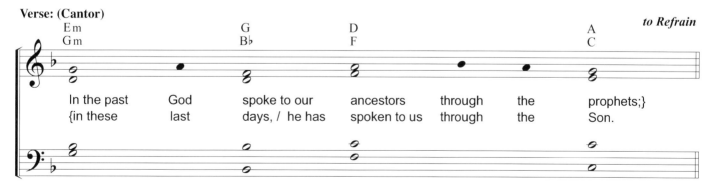

# The Holy Family of Jesus, Mary and Joseph

*Psalm for Years ABC*
*December 31*

Psalm 128:1-2, 3, 4-5, 6

*to Refrain*

of Je - ru - sa - lem      all the days ___ of your life.

**REFRAIN**

Bless-ed are      those who fear the Lord,      and walk in his ways.

**Note: Response reprinted for convenience**

**Gospel Acclamation**: Col 3: 15A, 16A
**Acclamation:** (Keyboard/SATB) NO. III

(M.M. ♩ = c. 160)

Al - le - lu - ia,      al - le - lu - ia.

**Verse: (Cantor)**                                        *to Refrain*

Let      the      peace of      Christ con - trol      your      hearts;}
{let      the      word of      Christ dwell      in      you      richly.

# Solemnity of Mary, the Holy Mother of God

*January 1*

**REFRAIN**

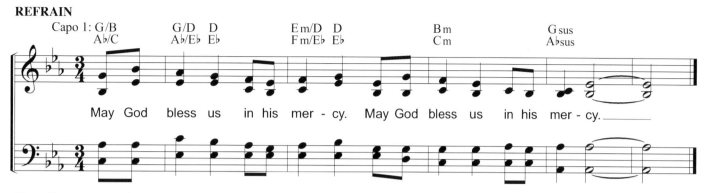

May God bless us in his mer-cy. May God bless us in his mer-cy.____

**Note: Response reprinted for convenience**

**Gospel Acclamation**: Hebrews 1:1-2

**Acclamation:** (Keyboard/SATB) NO. I

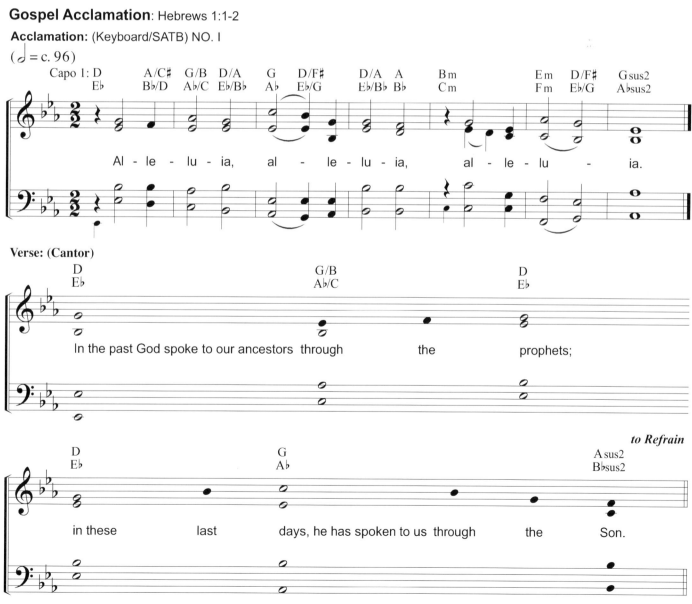

Al-le-lu-ia, al-le-lu-ia, al-le-lu-ia.

**Verse: (Cantor)**

In the past God spoke to our ancestors through the prophets;

*to Refrain*

in these last days, he has spoken to us through the Son.

# The Epiphany of the Lord

*January 7*

Psalm 72:1-2, 7-8, 10-11, 12-13

*to Refrain*

**Verse 4**

*to Refrain*

low - ly and the poor; the lives of the poor he shall save.

**REFRAIN**

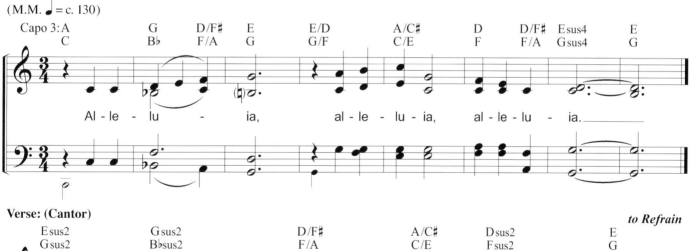

Lord, ev - 'ry na - tion on earth will a - dore you.

**Note: Response reprinted for convenience**

## Gospel Acclamation: Matthew 2:2

**Acclamation:** (Keyboard/SATB) NO. II

(M.M. ♩ = c. 130)

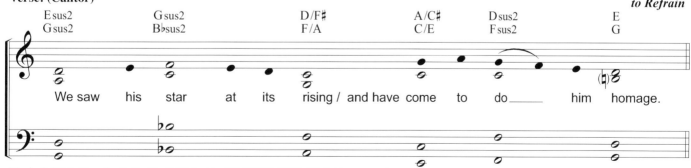

Al - le - lu - ia, al - le - lu - ia, al - le - lu - ia.

**Verse: (Cantor)**

*to Refrain*

We saw his star at its rising / and have come to do ____ him homage.

# Second Sunday in Ordinary Time

*January 14*

Psalm 40:2, 4, 7-8, 8-9, 10

**REFRAIN**

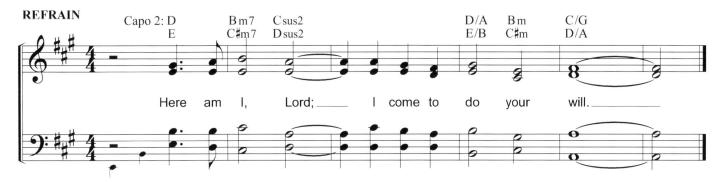

Here am I, Lord;____ I come to do your will.____

**Note: Response reprinted for convenience**

## Gospel Acclamation: John 1:41, 17b

**Acclamation:** (Keyboard/SATB) NO. V

(M.M. ♪ = c. 150)

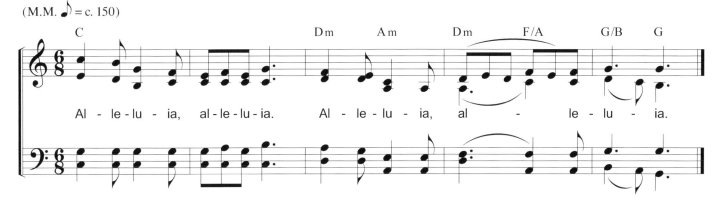

Al - le -lu - ia, al-le-lu-ia. Al - le - lu - ia, al - le - lu - ia.

**Verse: (Cantor)** *to Refrain*

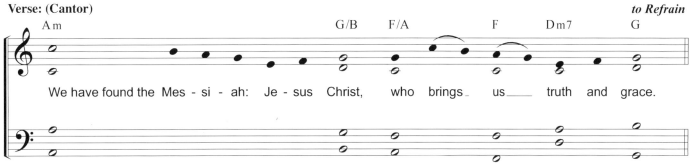

We have found the Mes - si - ah: Je - sus Christ, who brings__ us__ truth and grace.

# Third Sunday in Ordinary Time

*January 21*

Psalm 25:4–5, 6–7, 8–9

**Verse 2**

*to Refrain*

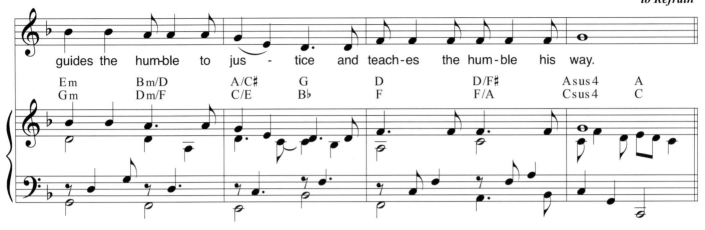

guides the hum-ble to jus - tice and teach-es the hum-ble his way.

**REFRAIN**

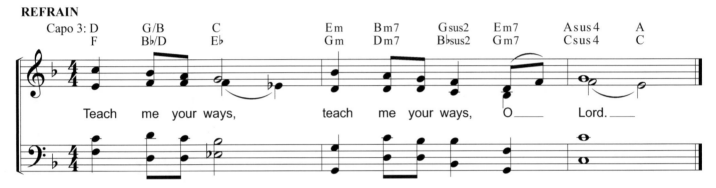

Teach me your ways, teach me your ways, O Lord.

Note: Response reprinted for convenience

## Gospel Acclamation: Mark 1:15
**Acclamation: (Keyboard/SATB) NO. III**

(M.M. ♩ = c. 160)

Al - le - lu - ia, al - le - lu - ia.

**Verse: (Cantor)**

The kingdom of God is at hand. / Re - pent and believe in the Gospel.

# Fourth Sunday in Ordinary Time

*January 28*

Psalm 95:1-2, 6-7, 7-9

**REFRAIN**
(M.M. ♩ = c. 100)

If to-day you hear his voice, hard - en not your hearts.

**Verse 1**

Come, let us sing joy-ful-ly to the LORD; let us ac-claim the rock of our sal - va - tion. Let us come in-to his pre-sence with thanks-giv-ing; let us joy-ful-ly sing psalms to him.

*to Refrain*

**Verse 2**

*to Refrain*

Come, let us bow down in wor - ship; let us kneel be - fore the LORD who made us.___ For he is our God, and we are the peop - le he shep-herds, the flock he guides.

**Verse 3**

Oh, that to - day_____ you would hear his voice:

**REFRAIN**

*Note: Response reprinted for convenience.*

**Gospel Acclamation**: Matthew 4:16

**Acclamation:** (Keyboard/SATB) NO. IV

Al-le - lu - ia,___ al-le-lu - ia,___ al-le-lu - ia. ia.

**Verse: (Cantor)**

The people who sit in darkness have seen a great light; / on those}
{dwelling in a land ov - er - shadowed by death, light has a - risen.

# Fifth Sunday in Ordinary Time

*February 4*

Psalm 147:1–2, 3–4, 5–6

**Verse 2**

He heals the bro - ken - heart - ed ___ and binds up their wounds. He
tells the num - ber of the stars; he calls each by name.

*to Refrain*

**Verse 3**

Great is our LORD and might - y in pow'er; to his wis - dom there is no lim - it. ___ The
LORD sus - tains the low - ly; ___ the wick - ed he casts to the ground.

*to Refrain*

**REFRAIN [or: Alleluia]**

Praise the Lord. Praise the Lord, who heals the bro-ken-heart-ed.

**Note: Response reprinted for convenience**

## Gospel Acclamation: Matthew 8:17

**Acclamation:** (Keyboard/SATB) NO. I

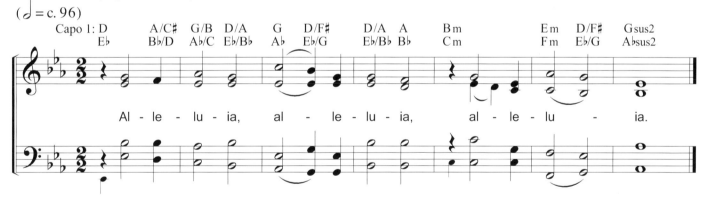

Al-le-lu-ia, al-le-lu-ia, al-le-lu-ia.

**Verse: (Cantor)**

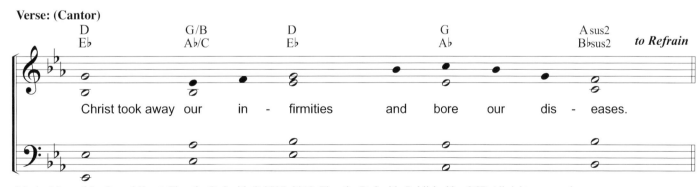

Christ took away our in-firmities and bore our dis-eases.

Music: Mass of the Sacred Heart; Timothy R. Smith © 2007, 2010, Timothy R. Smith. Published by OCP. All rights reserved.

# Sixth Sunday in Ordinary Time

*February 11*

Psalm 32:1-2, 5, 11

Gospel Acclamation: Luke 7:16

Acclamation: (Keyboard/SATB) NO. III

(M.M. ♩ = c. 160)

Al — le - lu — ia, al - le - lu — ia._____

Verse: (Cantor)

A great prophet has arisen in our midst, God has visited his people.

# Ash Wednesday

*February 14*

Psalm 51:3-4, 5-6ab, 12-13, 14 & 17

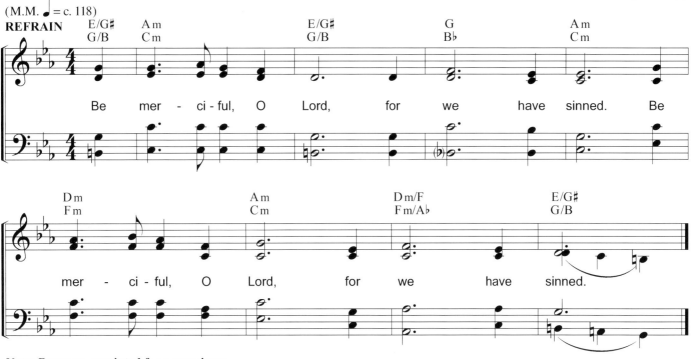

(M.M. ♩ = c. 118)

**REFRAIN**

Be mer - ci - ful, O Lord, for we have sinned. Be

mer - ci - ful, O Lord, for we have sinned.

**Note: Response reprinted for convenience.**

**Gospel Acclamation**: See Psalm 95:8

**Acclamation:** (Keyboard/SATB) NO. VII

(♩ = c. 90)

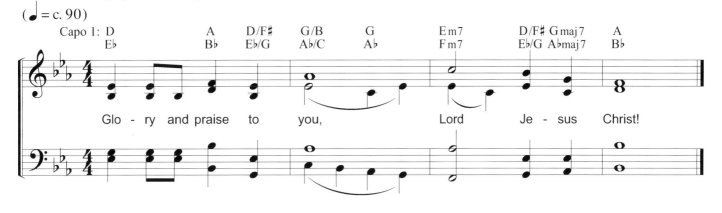

Glo - ry and praise to you, Lord Je - sus Christ!

**Verse: (Cantor)**                                                                 *to Refrain*

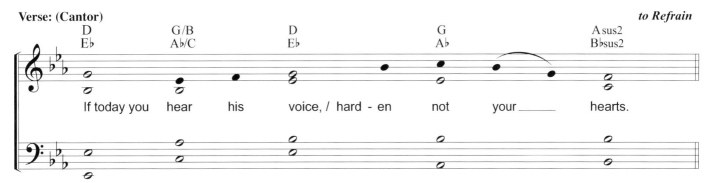

If today you hear his voice, / hard - en not your _____ hearts.

# First Sunday of Lent

*February 18*

Psalm 25:4–5, 6–7, 8–9

**Verse 2**

*to Refrain*

**Verse 3**

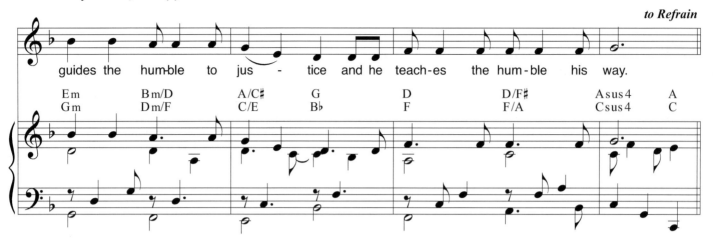

**REFRAIN**

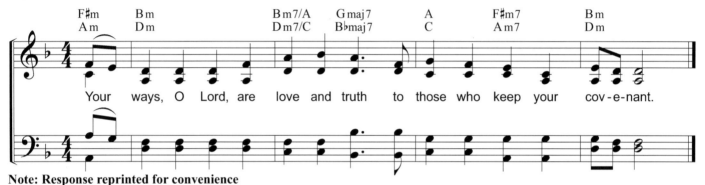

**Note: Response reprinted for convenience**

**Gospel Acclamation**: Matthew 4:4b

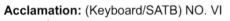

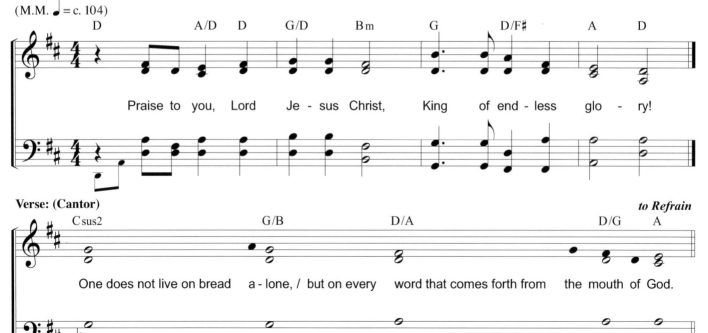

# Second Sunday of Lent

*February 25*

(M.M. ♩ = c. 72)

Psalm 116:10, 15, 16–17, 18–19

**REFRAIN**

I will walk be-fore the Lord, in the land of the liv-ing.

**Verse 1**

I be-lieved, e-ven when I said, "I am great-ly af-flict-ed."

*to Refrain*

Pre-cious in the eyes of the LORD is the death of his faith-ful ones.

**Verse 2**

O LORD, I am your ser-vant; I am your ser-vant, the son of your

**REFRAIN**

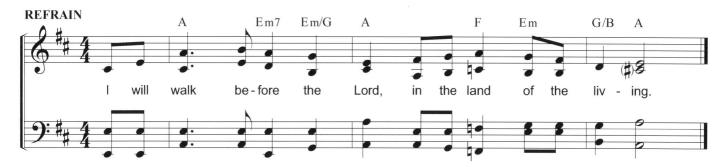

I will walk be-fore the Lord, in the land of the liv - ing.

Note: Response reprinted for convenience

## Gospel Acclamation: Matthew 17:5

**Acclamation:** (Keyboard/SATB) NO. VII

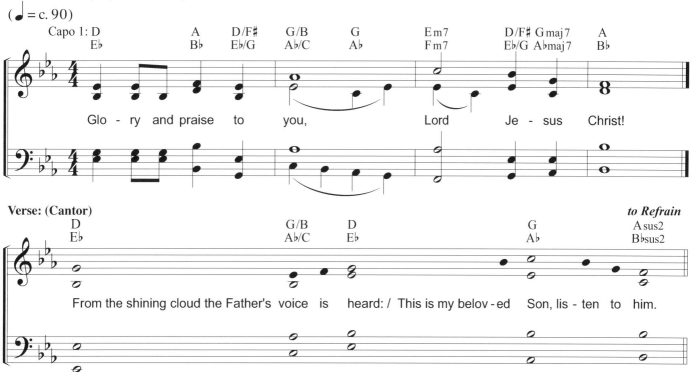

Glo - ry and praise to you, Lord Je - sus Christ!

**Verse:** (Cantor)                                                                 *to Refrain*

From the shining cloud the Father's voice is heard: / This is my belov-ed Son, lis-ten to him.

Music: *Mass of the Sacred Heart*; Timothy R. Smith, © 2007, 2010, Timothy R. Smith. Published by OCP. All rights reserved.

# Third Sunday of Lent

*March 3*

Psalm 19:8, 9, 10, 11

- er;___ the or - di - nanc - es___ of the LORD are___

Dmaj7/F#   Em   D/F#   G   Asus2   A

*to Refrain*

true,   all   of   them   just.

Bm   Csus2   Em7   A7sus4

**Verse 4**

They are more pre-cious than gold,   than a heap of pur - est gold;___

F   Dsus2   Fsus2   F   D

*to Refrain*

sweet - er al - so than syr-up___ or hon - ey from the comb.

F/C   G/B   Gm/B♭   F/A   Em7/G   Em7   A7sus4

*rit.*

86

**REFRAIN**

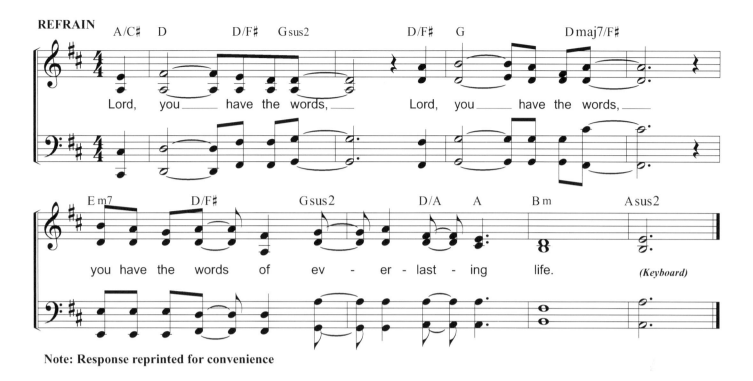

Lord, you have the words, Lord, you have the words, you have the words of ev - er - last - ing life.

*(Keyboard)*

**Note: Response reprinted for convenience**

**Gospel Acclamation**: John 3:16

**Acclamation:** (Keyboard/SATB) NO. VI

(M.M. ♩ = c. 104)

Praise to you, Lord, Je - sus Christ, King of end - less glo - ry!

**Verse: (Cantor)**

*to Refrain*

God so loved the world that he gave his on - ly Son, / so that}
{everyone who believes in him might have e - ter - nal life.

# RCIA Option: Third Sunday of Lent

*March 3*

Psalm 95:1-2, 6-7, 8-9

(M.M. ♩ = c. 100)

**REFRAIN**

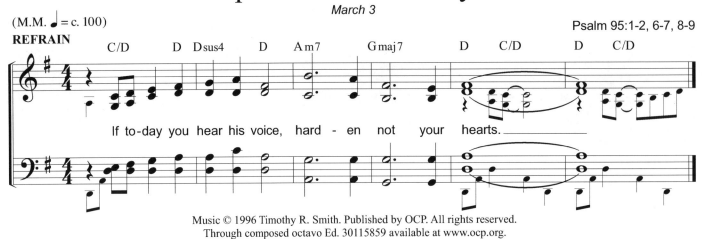

If to-day you hear his voice, hard-en not your hearts.

*Complete setting is on page 67*

**Gospel Acclamation**: cf. John 4:42, 15

**Acclamation:** (Keyboard/SATB) NO. VI

(M.M. ♩ = c. 104)

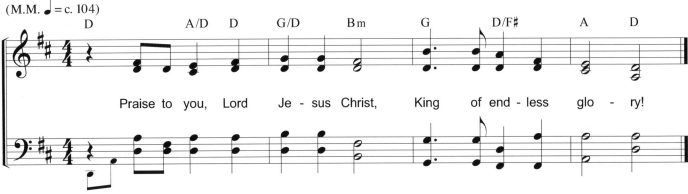

Praise to you, Lord Je-sus Christ, King of end-less glo-ry!

**Verse: (Cantor)**                                                                                          *to Refrain*

Lord, you are truly the Sav-ior of the world;}
{give me liv-ing water, / that I may nev-er thirst a-gain.

# Fourth Sunday of Lent

*March 10*

Psalm 137:1–2, 3, 4–5, 6

REFRAIN

(M.M. ♩ = c. 124)

Let my tongue be si-lenced, if I ev - er for-get you, ev - er for-get you! *(Keyboard)*

**Verse 1**

By the streams of Bab-y-lon we sat and wept when we re-mem-bered Zi - on. On the as-pens of that land we hung up our harps.

*to Refrain*

**Fourth Sunday of Lent, cont. (2)**

**Verse 2**

*to Refrain*

**Verse 3**

*to Refrain*

90

**Verse 4**

**REFRAIN**

**Note: Response reprinted for convenience**

## Gospel Acclamation: John 3:16

**Acclamation:** (Keyboard/SATB) NO. VII

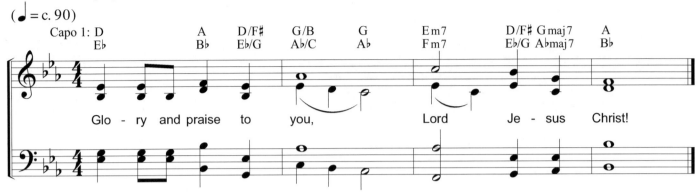

Glo - ry and praise to you, Lord Je - sus Christ!

**Verse: (Cantor)**                                        *to Refrain*

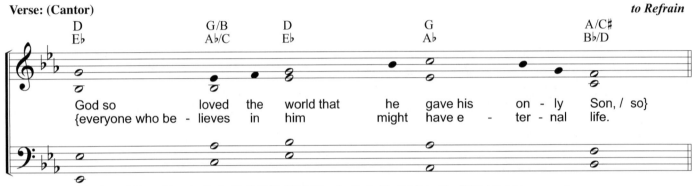

God so loved the world that he gave his on - ly Son, / so}
{everyone who be - lieves in him might have e - ter - nal life.

# RCIA Option: Fourth Sunday of Lent

*March 10*

Psalm 23:1-3a, 3b-4, 5, 6

(M.M. ♩ = c. 114)

**REFRAIN**

**Note: Response reprinted for convenience**

**Verse 4**

95

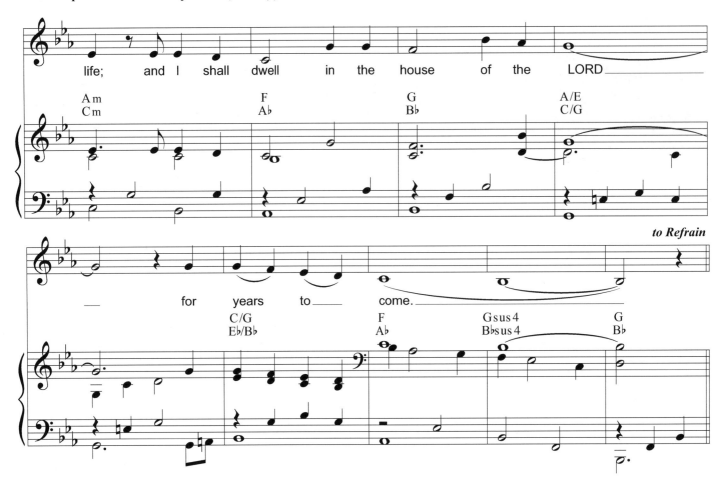

## Gospel Acclamation: John 8:12

**Acclamation:** (Keyboard/SATB) NO. VI

# Fifth Sunday of Lent
*March 17*

**Verse 2** (M.M. ♩ = c. 69)

A clean heart cre-ate for me, O God, and a stead-fast
spir-it re-new__ with-in me.__ Cast me not out from your
pres-ence, and your Ho-ly Spir-it take not from me.

*to Refrain*

**Verse 3** (M.M. ♩ = c. 69)

Give me back the joy of your sal-va-tion, and a will-ing

*to Refrain*

(M.M. ♩ = c. 77)
**REFRAIN**

**Note: Response reprinted for convenience.**

## Gospel Acclamation: John 12:26

**Acclamation:** (Keyboard/SATB) NO. VI

Praise to you, Lord, Je - sus Christ, King of end - less glor - y!

**Verse: (Cantor)**

Whoever serves me must follow me, says the Lord; / and}
{where I am, / there also will my ser - vant be.

# RCIA Option: Fifth Sunday of Lent

*March 17*

Psalm 130:1-2, 3-4, 5-6, 7-8

*to Refrain*

dawn, let Is - ra - el wait for the LORD.

**Verse 4**

For with the LORD is kind - ness and with him

is plen - te - ous re - demp - tion; and he will re - deem__

*to Refrain*

Is - ra - el from all their in - i - qui - ties.

*poco rit.*

**Gospel Acclamation**: John 11:25a, 26

**Acclamation:** (Keyboard/SATB) NO. VI

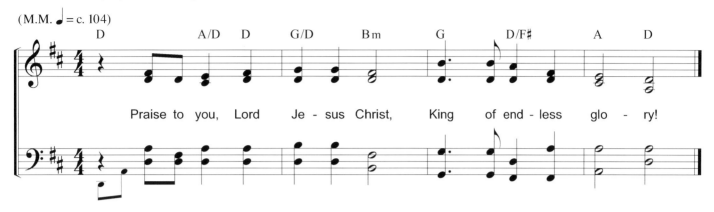

Praise to you, Lord Jesus Christ, King of endless glory!

**Verse: (Cantor)**

*to Refrain*

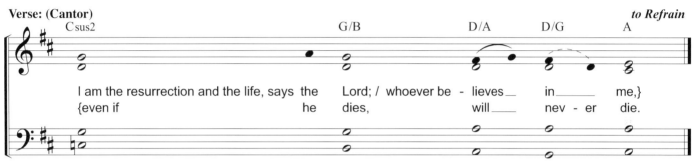

I am the resurrection and the life, says the Lord; / whoever believes in me,}
{even if he dies, will never die.

# Palm Sunday of the Passion of the Lord

*March 24*

(M.M. ♩ = c. 89)

Psalm 22:8-9, 17-18, 19-20, 23-24

**REFRAIN**

My God, my God, why have you a-ban-doned me?

**Verse 1**

All who see me scoff at me; they mock me with part-ed lips, they wag their heads: "He re-lied on the LORD; let him de-liv-er him, let him res-cue him, if he loves him."

*to Refrain*

106

**Verse 2**

In-deed, man-y dogs sur-round me, a pack of ev-il-do-ers
Bm F#m Gsus2 Bm F#m
Dm Am Bbsus2 Dm Am

clos-es in u-pon___ me; they have pierced my
Gsus2 Bm F#m/A
Bbsus2 Dm Am/C

*to Refrain*

hands and my feet; I can count all my bones.
G D/F# Em7 Bm
Bb F/A Gm7 Dm

**Verse 3**

They div-ide my gar-ments___ a-mong them, and for my
Bm F#m Gsus2 Bm
Dm Am Bbsus2 Dm

praise him; all you des-cen-dants of Jac-ob, give glo-ry to

C / E♭ — B m / D m — F♯m/A / A m/C — G / B♭ — D/F♯ / F/A — E m7 / G m7

him; re-vere him, all you des-cen-dants of Is-ra-el!"

B m / D m — B m / D m — F♯m/A / A m/C — E m7 / G m7 — B m / D m

**REFRAIN**

Capo 3: B m / D m — F♯m/A / A m/C — G maj7 / B♭maj7 — F♯m7 / A m7 — E m7 / G m7 — B m / D m | 1st time

My God, my God, why have you a-ban-doned me?

**Note: Response reprinted for convenience**

## Gospel Acclamation: Philippians 2:8-9
**Acclamation:** (Keyboard/SATB) NO. VII

**Verse: (Cantor)**

Glo - ry and praise to you, Lord Je - sus Christ!

Christ became obedient to the point of death,
{Because of this, / God greatly ex - alted him

*to Refrain*

ev - en death on a cross.}
and bestowed on him the name which is above ev - 'ry name.

# Thursday of the Lord's Supper (Holy Thursday):
## At the Evening Mass
*March 28*

Psalm 116:12-13,15-16bc, 17-18

*to Refrain*

**Verse 3**

**Note: Response reprinted for convenience**

## Gospel Acclamation: John 13:34

**Acclamation:** (Keyboard/SATB) NO. VII

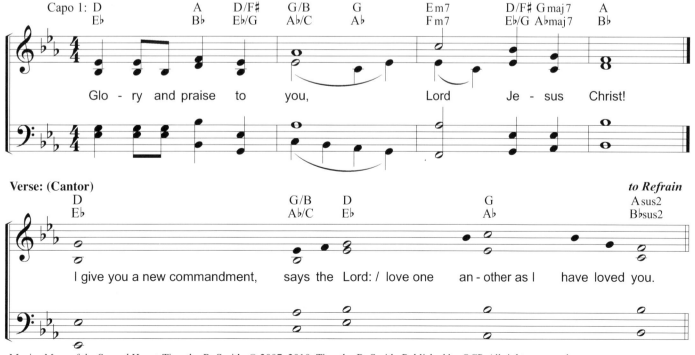

# Friday of the Passion of the Lord (Good Friday)

*March 29*

Psalm 31:2, 6, 12-13, 15-16, 17, 25

**Verse 2**

*to Refrain*

**Verse 3**

*to Refrain*

**REFRAIN**

**Note: Response reprinted for convenience**

**Verse 4**

Let your face shine up - on your ser - vant; save me in your kind - ness.

Take cour - age and be stout - heart - ed, all you who

*to Refrain*

hope in the LORD, [all you who hope in the LORD. _____

## Gospel Acclamation: Philippians 2:8-9

**Acclamation:** (Keyboard/SATB) NO. VII

Glo - ry and praise to you, Lord Je - sus Christ!

**Verse:** (Cantor)

Christ became obedient to the point of death,
{Because of this, / God greatly ex - alted him

*to Refrain*

ev - en death on a cross.}
and bestowed on him the name which is above every oth - er name.

# The Easter Vigil in the Holy Night

**Responsorial Psalm (following first reading)** *March 30*

(M.M. ♩ = c. 116)

Psalm 104:1-2, 5-6, 10, 12, 13-14, 24, 35

Lord, send out your Spir - it, and re-new the face of the earth.

**Verse 1**

Bless the LORD, O my soul! O LORD, my God, you are great in-deed! You are clothed with maj - es-ty and glo-ry, robed in light as with a cloak.

*to Refrain* **Verse 2**

You fixed the earth up-on its foun - da-tion, not to be

**Verse 5**

Note: Response reprinted for convenience.

Alternate Responsorial Psalm (following first reading)

*to Refrain*

**Verse 3**

125

**Note: Response reprinted for convenience.**

**Responsorial Psalm (following second reading)**

(M.M. ♩ = c. 106)

Psalm 16:5, 8, 9-10, 11

**REFRAIN**

**Verse 1**

*to Refrain*

**Verse 2**

**Note: Response reprinted for convenience.**

## Responsorial Psalm (following third reading)

(M.M. ♩ = c. 92)

Exodus 15:1-2, 3-4, 5-6, 17-18

**REFRAIN**

Capo 3: Asus2 / Csus2  G/B / Bb/D  D / F  Asus2 / Csus2  Dm / Fm  Dm/F / Fm/Ab  G / Bb  Asus2 / Csus2

Let us sing to the Lord; he has cov-ered him-self in glo - ry.

**Verse 1**

I will sing to the LORD, for he is glo-ri-ous-ly tri-um-phant; horse and

Asus2 / Csus2    G/A / Bb/C   D/A / F/C   Asus4 / Csus4

char - iot he has cast in - to the sea. My strength and my cour - age

G/A / Bb/C   D/A / F/C   Asus2 / Csus2   Dm / Fm   Dm/F / Fm/Ab

is the LORD, and he has been my sav - ior. He is my God, I

G / Bb   Em7 / Gm7   Asus2 / Csus2   G/A / Bb/C

Note: Response reprinted for convenience.

**Responsorial Psalm (following fourth reading)**

(M.M. ♩ = c. 118)

Psalm 30:2, 4, 5-6, 11-12, 13

**REFRAIN**

**Verse 1**

**Verse 2**

**Verse 3**

**REFRAIN**

Note: Response reprinted for convenience.

**Responsorial Psalm (following fifth reading)**

(M.M. ♩ = c. 120)

**REFRAIN**

Isaiah 12:2-3, 4bcd, 5-6

**Verse 1**

*to Refrain*

joy you will draw wa - ter at the foun - tain of sal - va - tion._____

C/E      B m/D      C      A sus 4
D/F♯      C♯m/E      D      B sus 4

**Verse 2**

Give thanks to the LORD, ac - claim his name; a - mong the

A sus 4      D      C/D      D
B sus 4      E      D/E      E

na - tions make known his deeds, pro - claim how ex -

D/F♯      G sus 2      A sus 4      E m
E/G♯      A sus 2      B sus 4      F♯m

*to Refrain*

alt - ed_____ is his name._____

B m/D      C      G/B      A sus 4
C♯m/E      D      A/C♯      B sus 4

**Verse 3**

Note: Response reprinted for convenience.

**Responsorial Psalm (following sixth reading)**

(M.M. ♩ = c. 124)

Psalm 19:8, 9, 10, 11

**REFRAIN**

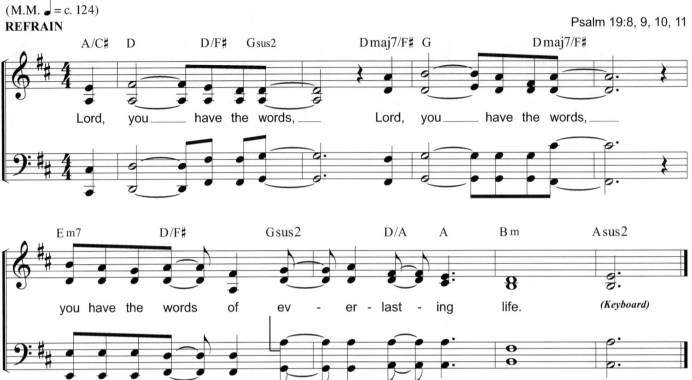

Lord, you have the words, Lord, you have the words, you have the words of ev - er - last - ing life. (Keyboard)

*Complete setting is on page 84*

*Option A,* when Baptism is celebrated
**Responsorial Psalm (following seventh reading)**

Psalm 42:3, 5; 43:3, 4

(M.M. ♩ = c. 64)
**REFRAIN**

**Verse 2**

*to Refrain*

I went with the throng and led them in pro-ces-sion to the house of __ God, a-mid loud cries of joy __ and thanks-giv-ing, __ with the mul-ti-tude keep-ing fes-ti-val.

**Verse 3**

*to Refrain*

Send forth your light and your fi-del-i-ty; they shall lead me on and bring me to your ho-ly moun-tain, __ to your dwell-ing-place.

**Verse 4**

*to Refrain*

**REFRAIN**

Note: Response reprinted for convenience

**The Easter Vigil in the Holy Night, cont. (26)**
*Or: Option B,* when Baptism is not celebrated
**Responsorial Psalm (following seventh reading)**

(M.M. ♩ = c. 120)
**REFRAIN**

Isaiah 12:2-3, 4bcd, 5-6

You will draw wat - er joy - ful - ly_____ from the

springs of _____ sal - va - tion. _____

© 2013, Timothy R. Smith. Published by TR TUNE, LLC. All rights reserved.
www.timothyrsmith.com

*Complete setting is on page 139*

146

*Or: Option C,* when Baptism is not celebrated
**Responsorial Psalm (following seventh reading)**
(M.M. ♩ = c. 77)
**REFRAIN**

Psalm 51:12-13, 14-15, 18-19

Cre-ate _____ a clean heart, a clean heart in me, O God.

**Verse 1** (M.M. ♩ = c. 69)

A clean heart cre-ate for me, O God, and a stead-fast

spir-it re-new _____ with-in me. _____ Cast me not out from your

*to Refrain*

pres-ence, and your Ho-ly Spir-it take not from me.

**Verse 2** (M.M. ♩ = c. 69)

Give me back the joy of your sal - va - tion, and a will - ing spir - it sus - tain___ in me. I will teach trans - gres - sors your ways, and___ sin - ners shall re - turn to you.

*to Refrain*

**Verse 3** (M.M. ♩ = c. 69)

For you are not pleased with sac - ri - fic - es;___ should I of - fer a hol - o - caust,

*to Refrain*

(M.M. ♩ = c. 77)
**REFRAIN**

**Note: Response reprinted for convenience.**

**Responsorial Psalm**: Psalm 118:1-2, 16-17, 22-23
**Acclamation**: (Keyboard/SATB) NO. II

(M.M. ♩ = c. 154)

**REFRAIN**

Al - le - lu - ia, al - le - lu - ia, al - le - lu - ia.

**Verse 1**

Give thanks to the LORD, for he is good, for his mer-cy en-

dures for - ev - er. Let the house of Is - ra - el

*to Refrain*

say, "His mer-cy en-dures for - ev - er." _____

**Verse 2**

The Easter Vigil in the Holy Night, cont. (31)

"The right hand of the LORD has struck with pow'r; the right hand of the

LORD is ex - alt - ed._____ I shall not die, but live,_____

*to Refrain*

and de - clare___ the works_____ of the LORD."_____

**Verse 3**

The stone which the build - ers re - ject - ed has be - come the

**Note: Response reprinted for convenience**

# Easter Sunday of the Resurrection of the Lord: At the Mass during the Day

REFRAIN [or: Alleluia]

*Macrh 31*

Psalm 118:1-2, 16-17, 22-23

This is the day the Lord has made; let us re- joice and be glad.

**Verse 1**

Give thanks to the LORD, for he is good, for his mer- cy en-

dures for - ev - er. Let the house of Is - ra - el

*to Refrain*

say, "His mer- cy en- dures for - ev - er."

**Verse 2**

cor - ner - stone. _____ By \_\_ the LORD has this been

done; it is won - der - ful in our eyes. _____

*to Refrain*

**REFRAIN [or: Alleluia]**

This is the day the Lord has \_\_ made; let us re - joice and be glad. \_\_\_\_\_

**Gospel Acclamation**: cf. 1 Corinthians 5:7b-8a

**Acclamation:** (Keyboard/SATB) NO. V

(M.M. ♪ = c. 150)

Al - le - lu - ia, al - le - lu - ia. Al - le - lu - ia, al - le - lu - ia.

**Verse:** (Cantor)

*to Refrain*

Christ, our pas - chal lamb, has been sacrificed; let us then feast with joy in the Lord.

# Second Sunday of Easter (or Sunday of Divine Mercy)

*April 7*

(M.M. ♩ = c. 114)

Psalm 118:2-4, 13-15, 22-24

*to Refrain*

**Verse 2**

157

*to Refrain*

**Verse 3**

By the LORD_____ has__ this___ been done; [it is

won - der - ful,]_____ it is won - der - ful in____ our___ eyes.

This is the day the____ LORD has____ made;

*to Refrain*

let us be___ glad and re - joice in it.___

**REFRAIN [or: Alleluia]**

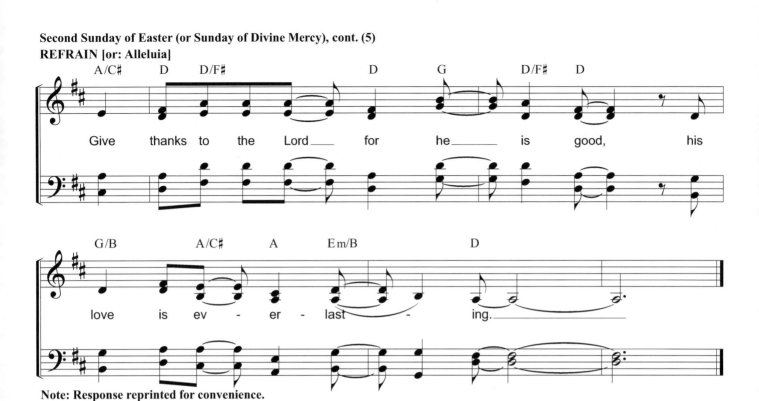

Give thanks to the Lord for he is good, his love is ev - er - last - ing.

**Note: Response reprinted for convenience.**

## Gospel Acclamation: John 20:29

**Acclamation:** (Keyboard/SATB) NO. III

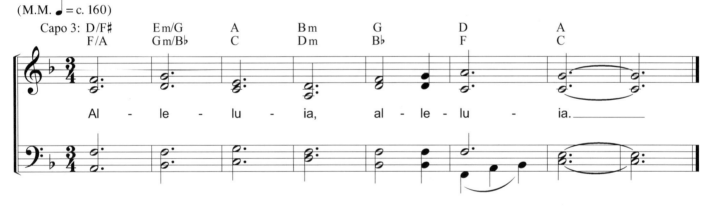

Al - le - lu - ia, al - le - lu - ia.

**Verse: (Cantor)**

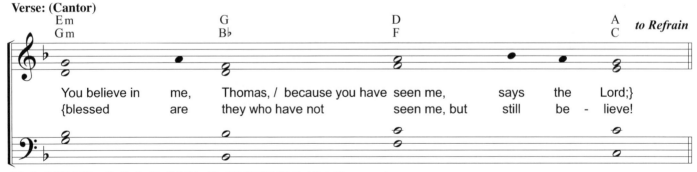

You believe in me, Thomas, / because you have seen me, says the Lord;}
{blessed are they who have not seen me, but still be - lieve!

# Third Sunday of Easter

*April 14*

**Verse 2**

*to Refrain*

**Verse 3**

*to Refrain*

**Verse 4**

As soon as I lie down, I fall peace-ful-ly a-sleep, for you a-lone, O LORD, bring se-

*to Refrain*

cu - ri - ty to my dwell - ing.

**Gospel Acclamation**: Luke 24:32

**Acclamation:** (Keyboard/SATB) NO. III

(M.M. ♩ = c. 160)

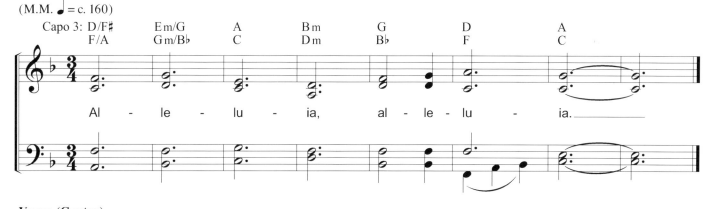

Al - le - lu - ia, al - le - lu - ia.

**Verse: (Cantor)**

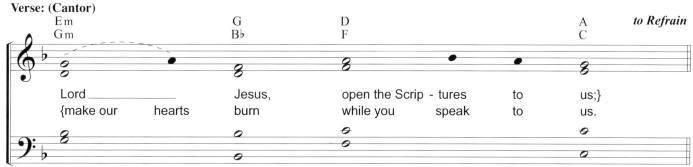

Lord _____ Jesus, open the Scrip - tures to us;}
{make our hearts burn while you speak to us.

*to Refrain*

# Fourth Sunday of Easter

*April 21*

(M.M. ♩ = c. 75)

Psalm 118:1, 8–9, 21–23, 26, 28, 29

**REFRAIN [or: Alleluia]**

The stone re-jec-ted by the build-ers has be-come the cor-ner - stone.

**Verse 1**

Give thanks to the LORD, for he is good, for his mer-cy en-dures for-

ev-er.___ It is bet-ter to take ref-uge in the LORD than to trust in

man. It is bet-ter to take ref-uge in the LORD than to trust in princ-es.___

*to Refrain*

*to Refrain*

**REFRAIN [or: Alleluia]**

**Gospel Acclamation**: John 10:14

**Acclamation:** (Keyboard/SATB) NO. IV

(M.M. ♩ = c. 116)

**Verse: (Cantor)**

*to Refrain*

# Fifth Sunday of Easter

*April 28*

Psalm 22:26–27, 28, 30, 31–32

REFRAIN [or: Alleluia]

I will praise you, Lord, _____ in the as - sem - bly of your peo - ple.

Verse 1

I will ful - fill my vows be - fore those who fear the LORD. The low - ly shall eat their fill; they who seek the LORD shall praise him: "May your hearts live for - ev - er!"

*to Refrain*

**Verse 2** (M.M. ♩ = c. 62)

All the ends of the earth shall re - mem - ber and turn to the

E/G♯  Am  C7/G  Fsus4  F  Fm  C/G  D7/G

*to Refrain*

LORD; all the fam - 'lies of the na - tions shall bow down be - fore him.

G7sus4  E/G♯  Am  C7/G  Fsus4  F  F/A♭  C/G  D7/G  G7sus4

**Verse 3** (M.M. ♩ = c. 62)

To __ him a - lone shall bow down all who sleep in the earth; be -

E/G♯  Am  C7/G  Fsus4  F  Fm  C/G  D7/G  G7sus4  E/G♯

*to Refrain*

fore him shall bend all who __ go down in - to the dust.

Am  C7/G  F  Fm/A♭  C/G  D7/G  G7sus4

**Verse 4**  (M.M. ♩ = c. 62)

**REFRAIN [or: Alleluia]**

I will praise you, Lord, _____ in the as - sem - bly of your peo - ple.

**Note: Response reprinted for convenience**

## Gospel Acclamation: John 15:4a, 5b

**Acclamation:** (Keyboard/SATB) NO. IV

**Verse:** (Cantor)

*to Refrain*

Remain in me   as      I remain      in       you,      says      the      Lord. / Who –
{ever     re –    mains      in       me will     bear      much     fruit.

# Sixth Sunday of Easter

*May 5*

Psalm 98:1, 2-3, 3-4

(M.M. ♩ = c. 146)

**REFRAIN [or: Alleluia]**

**Verse 1**

*to Refrain*

**Verse 2**

The LORD has made his sal - va - tion known: in the sight of the na - tions he has re - vealed his jus - tice. He has re - mem - bered his kind - ness and his faith - ful - ness toward the house of Is - ra - el.

*to Refrain*

**Verse 3**

All __ the ends of the earth __ have seen the sal -

172

*to Refrain*

**REFRAIN [or: Alleluia]**

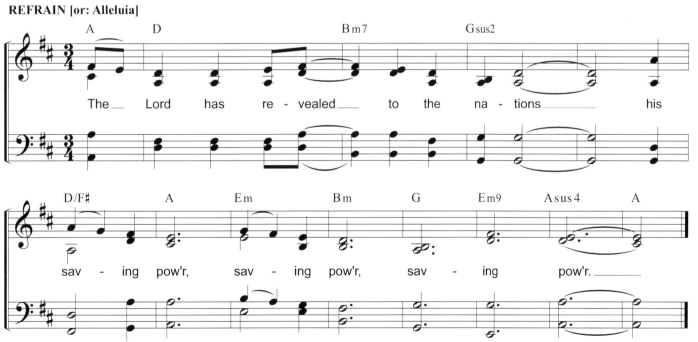

**Note: Response reprinted for convenience**

**Gospel Acclamation**: John 14:23

**Acclamation:** (Keyboard/SATB) NO. II

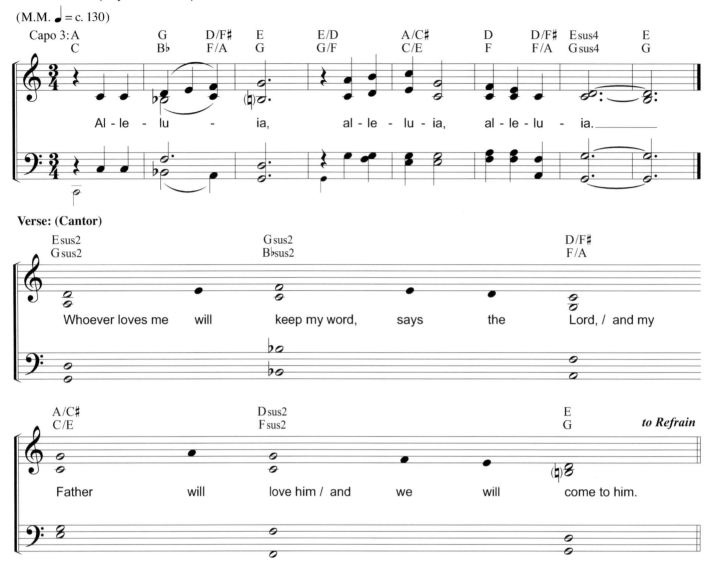

Al - le - lu - ia, al - le - lu - ia, al - le - lu - ia.

**Verse: (Cantor)**

Whoever loves me will keep my word, says the Lord, / and my

Father will love him / and we will come to him.

*to Refrain*

# The Ascension of the Lord

*May 9*

*The Ascension of the Lord* may be celebrated on Thursday May 9 or transferred
to Sunday May 12, depending upon the practice of each province.

Psalm 47:2-3, 6-7, 8-9

**Verse 2**

*to Refrain*

**Verse 3**

*to Refrain*

**REFRAIN [or: Alleluia]**

**Note: Response reprinted for convenience**

**Gospel Acclamation**: Matthew 28:19a, 20b
**Acclamation:** (Keyboard/SATB) NO. III

**Verse: (Cantor)**

Go and teach all nations, says the Lord;}
{I am with you always, / until the end of the world.

*to Refrain*

# Seventh Sunday of Easter
*May 12*

Music © 2007, Timothy R. Smith. Published by OCP. All rights reserved.
Through composed octavo Ed. 30100716, available at www.ocp.org.

**Verse 2**

*to Refrain*

**Verse 3**

180

*to Refrain*

**REFRAIN [or: Alleluia]**

**Note: Response reprinted for convenience**

**Gospel Acclamation**: cf. John 14:18

**Acclamation:** (Keyboard/SATB) NO. IV

(M.M. ♩ = c. 116)

Al-le - lu - ia,___ al-le - lu - ia,___ al-le - lu - ia.   ia.

**Verse: (Cantor)**

I will not leave you orphans, / says the Lord. / I will come back to you, / and your}
{hearts will re - joice.

# Pentecost Sunday: At the Vigil Mass
## (Extended Form)
### *May 18*

Psalm 33:10-11, 12-13, 14-15

*to Refrain*

**Verse 2**

**REFRAIN**

**Note: Response reprinted for convenience**

Option 1:

**Responsorial Psalm (following second reading)**

(M.M. ♩ = c. 74)

Daniel 3:52, 53, 54, 55, 56

**REFRAIN**

Glo-ry and praise, glo-ry and praise, glo-ry and praise for ev-er!

**Verse 1**

"Bless-ed are you, O Lord, the God of our fa-thers, praise-wor-thy and ex-alt-ed a-bove all for-ev-er; And bless-ed is your ho-ly and glo-rious name, praise-wor-thy and ex-alt-ed a-bove all for all ag-es."

*to Refrain*

**Verse 2**

"Bless - ed are you in the tem - ple of your ho - ly glo - ry,

G    Bm    D    G    D

*to Refrain*

praise - wor - thy and ___ glo - rious a - bove ___ all for - ev - er."

Em    A/C#    D    A    F#m7    G

**Verse 3**

"Bless - ed are you on the throne of your King - dom, ___

G    D    A/C#    G/B    D/A

*to Refrain*

praise - wor - thy and ex - alt - ed a - bove all for - ev - er."

Em    A/C#    D    A    F#m7    G

**Verse 4**

"Bless-ed are you who look in - to the depths from your throne up-on the

cher - u - bim, praise-wor - thy and ex - alt-ed a - bove all for - ev - er."

*to Refrain*

**Verse 5**

"Bless - ed are you in the fir - ma-ment of heav - en,

praise - wor - thy and glo - ri - ous for - ev - er."

*to Refrain*

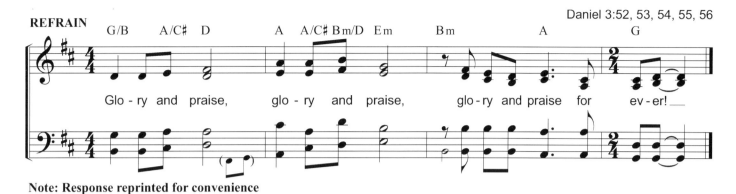

Daniel 3:52, 53, 54, 55, 56

REFRAIN

Glo-ry and praise, glo-ry and praise, glo-ry and praise for ev-er!

**Note: Response reprinted for convenience**

Option 2:

**Responsorial Psalm (following second reading)**

(M.M. ♩ = c. 124)

REFRAIN

Psalm 19:8, 9, 10, 11

Lord, you have the words, Lord, you have the words,

you have the words of ev - er - last - ing life.

*(Keyboard)*

Music © 2007, Timothy R. Smith. Published by OCP. All rights reserved.
Through composed octavo Ed. 30100583 available at www.ocp.org.

*Complete setting is on page 87*

**Responsorial Psalm (following third reading)**

(M.M. ♩ = c. 136)

Psalm 107:2-3, 4-5, 6-7, 8-9

**REFRAIN [or: Alleluia]**

**Verse 1**

*to Refrain*

**REFRAIN [or: Alleluia]**

**Note: Response reprinted for convenience.**

**Responsorial Psalm (following fourth reading)**

(M.M. ♩ = c. 116)

Psalm 104:1-2, 24 & 35, 27-28, 29, 30

**REFRAIN [or: Alleluia]**

Lord, send out your Spir-it, and re-new the face of the earth.

**Verse 1**

Bless the LORD, O my soul! O LORD, my God, you are great in-deed! You are clothed with maj-es-ty and glo-ry, robed in light as with a cloak.

*to Refrain*

**Verse 2**

How man - i - fold are your works, O LORD! In__ wis-dom you have wrought them all— the earth is full of your crea-tures; bless the LORD, O my soul! Al - le - lu - ia.___

*to Refrain*

**Verse 3**

Crea-tures all look to you to give them food in due

*to Refrain*

at - ed,___ and you re - new the face of the earth.

Gsus2    C/E    Gsus2    Gsus4    G

**REFRAIN [or: Alleluia]**

D    C/D    D    Bm7    C    D

Lord, send out___ your Spir - it,___ and re - new the face of the earth.___

**Note: Response reprinted for convenience.**

## Gospel Acclamation:

**Acclamation:** (Keyboard/SATB) NO. V

(M.M. ♩ = c. 150)

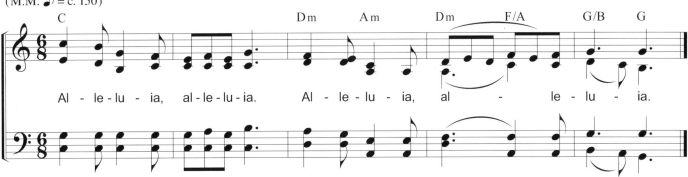

C    Dm    Am    Dm    F/A    G/B    G

Al - le - lu - ia, al - le - lu - ia. Al - le - lu - ia, al - le - lu - ia.

**Verse:** (Cantor)    *to Refrain*

Am    G/B    F/A    F    Dm9    G

Come, Holy Spirit, fill the hearts of your faithful / and kin - dle in them the fire of your love.

# Pentecost Sunday: At the Mass during the Day

*May 19*

(M.M. ♩ = c. 116)

**REFRAIN [or: Alleluia]**

Psalm 104:1, 24, 29-30, 31, 34

Lord, send out your Spir - it, and re-new the face of the earth.

**Verse 1**

Bless the LORD, O my soul! O LORD, my God, you are great in - deed! How man - i - fold are your works, O LORD! the earth is full of your crea - tures.

*to Refrain*

ev - er; may the LORD be glad in his works! Pleas-ing to him be my

*to Refrain*

theme; I will be glad in the LORD.

**REFRAIN [or: Alleluia]**

Lord, send out _____ your Spir - it, _____ and re-new the face of the earth.

**Note: Response reprinted for convenience.**

## Gospel Acclamation:

**Acclamation:** (Keyboard/SATB) NO. V

(M.M. ♪ = c. 150)

Al - le-lu - ia, al-le-lu - ia. Al - le-lu - ia, al - le-lu - ia.

**Verse: (Cantor)**

*to Refrain*

Come, Holy Spirit, fill the hearts of your faithful / and kin - dle in them the fire of your love.

# The Most Holy Trinity

*May 26*

Psalm 33:4–5, 6, 9, 18–19, 20, 22

**Verse 3**

*to Refrain*

**REFRAIN**

Alternate ending

Bless - ed the peo - ple the Lord has chos - en, the Lord has chos - en to be his own.

**Note: Response reprinted for convenience**

**Verse 4**

Our soul__ waits for the LORD, who is our help and our shield.__ May your

kind-ness, O LORD, be up-on us__ who have put our hope in__ you.

*to Refrain*

**REFRAIN**

Alternate ending

Bless-ed the peo-ple the Lord has chos-en, the Lord has chos-en to be his own.

Optional Interlude before Verse 3 & after final Refrain

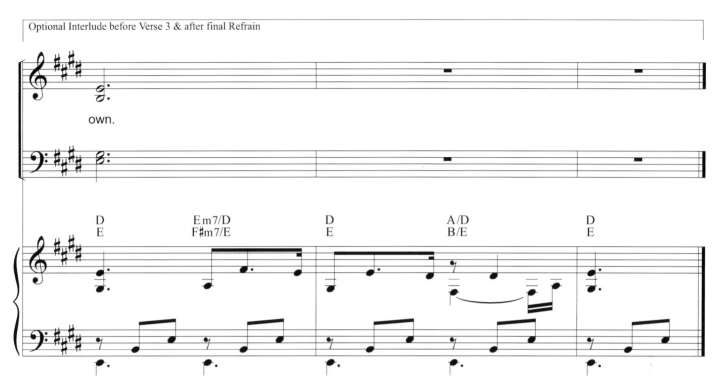

**Note: Response reprinted for convenience**

## Gospel Acclamation: cf. Revelation 1:8

**Acclamation:** (Keyboard/SATB) NO. I

Al - le - lu - ia, al - le - lu - ia, al - le - lu - ia.

**Verse: (Cantor)**

Glory to the Father, the Son, and the Ho - ly   Spirit; / to God who is,  who was, / and who is  to come.

# The Most Holy Body and Blood of Christ
## (Corpus Christi)
*June 2*

Psalm 116:12-13, 15-16, 17-18

(M.M. ♩ = c. 65)

**REFRAIN [or: Alleluia]**

I will take the cup of sal-va-tion, and call on the name of the Lord.

**Verse 1**

How shall I make a re-turn to the LORD for all the good he has done for me? The cup of sal-va-tion

*to Refrain*

I will take up, and I will call up-on the name of the LORD.

G/B    A    G    D    Asus4    A
B♭/D   C    B♭   F    Csus4    C

**Verse 2**

Pre - cious in the eyes of the LORD is the

Em    G/B    A    G
Gm    B♭/D   C    B♭

death of his faith - ful ones. I am your ser - vant, the

D    Asus4    A    Em    Bm/D
F    Csus4    C    Gm    Dm/F

*to Refrain*

son of your hand-maid; you have loosed my bonds.

G/B    A    G    D    Asus4    A
B♭/D   C    B♭   F    Csus4    C

**Verse 3**

**REFRAIN [or: Alleluia]**

I will take the cup of sal- va- tion, and call on the name of the Lord.

**Note: Response reprinted for convenience**

## Gospel Acclamation: John 6:51

**Acclamation: (Keyboard/SATB) NO. II**

(M.M. ♩ = c. 130)

Al - le - lu - ia, al - le - lu - ia, al - le - lu - ia.

**Verse: (Cantor)**

I am the living bread that came down from heaven, says the Lord; / whoever

eats this bread will live for - ever.

*to Refrain*

# 10th Sunday in Ordinary Time

*June 9*

Psalm 130:1-2, 3-4, 5-6, 7-8

With the Lord there is mer-cy and full-ness of _____ re-demp-tion.

*(Keyboard)*

**Complete setting is on page 102**

## Gospel Acclamation: John 12:31b–32

**Acclamation:** (Keyboard/SATB) NO. I

Al - le - lu - ia, al - le - lu - ia, al - le - lu - ia.

**Verse: (Cantor)**                                                                 *to Refrain*

Now the ruler        of    this  world will be driv - en   out,        says   the  Lord; / and}
{when I am lifted up    from  the   earth, / I will        draw  everyone      to    my - self.

# 11th Sunday in Ordinary Time

*June 16*

Psalm 92:2–3, 13–14, 15–16

(M.M. ♩ = c. 72)

**REFRAIN**

**NOTE: Refrain Vocals SAB in Treble Clef**

Lord, it is good to give thanks, give thanks to you.

Lord, it is good to give thanks, give thanks to you.

**Verse 1**

It is good to give thanks to the LORD, to sing praise to your name, Most High, to pro-claim your kind-ness at dawn and your

**Verse 3**

They shall bear___ fruit                    e - ven  in  old  age;___

vig - or-ous  and  stur-dy  shall  they  be,    de - clar-ing    how  just   is   the

*to Refrain*

LORD,    my rock,    in  whom there        is  no  wrong.

**REFRAIN**

*NOTE: Refrain Vocals SAB in Treble Clef*

Note: Response reprinted for convenience

## Gospel Acclamation:

**Acclamation:** (Keyboard/SATB) NO. IV

# 12th Sunday in Ordinary Time

*June 23*

(M.M. ♩ = c. 132)

Psalm 107:23-24, 25-26, 28-29, 30-31

**REFRAIN [or: Alleluia]**

Give__ thanks to the Lord;__ his love is ev - er -
last - ing,__ his love is ev - er - last - ing.

**Verse 1**

They who sailed the sea in ships, trad-ing on the deep wa-ters,__
these saw the works of the LORD and his won-ders in the a - byss.

*to Refrain*

**Verse 2**

His com-mand raised up a storm wind _____ which tossed its waves on

high. _____ They mount-ed up to heav-en; _____ they sank to the depths; _____

*to Refrain*

_____ their hearts melt-ed a - way in their plight. _____

**Verse 3**

They cried to the LORD in their dis-tress; from their straits he

*to Refrain*

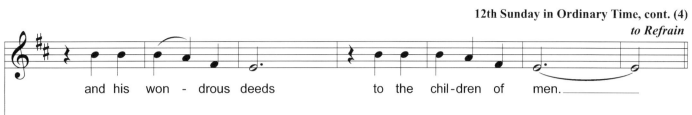

and his won - drous deeds    to the chil-dren of men.____

**REFRAIN**

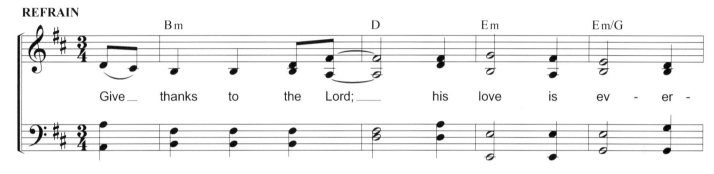

Give___ thanks  to  the  Lord;____  his  love  is  ev - er -

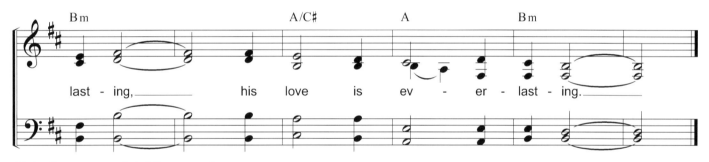

last - ing,_____  his  love  is  ev - er - last - ing.____

Note: Response reprinted for convenience.

## Gospel Acclamation: Luke 7:16

**Acclamation:** (Keyboard/SATB) NO. IV

**Verse: (Cantor)**

A great proph - et has risen in our midst.}
{God has visited his people.

*to Refrain*

# 13th Sunday in Ordinary Time

*June 30*

Psalm 30:2, 4, 5-6, 11-12, 13

(M.M. ♩ = c. 118)

REFRAIN

Bm  Gmaj7   A   F#m7   G

I will praise you, ___ Lord, for you have res - cued me. ___

***Complete setting is on page 136***

## Gospel Acclamation: cf. 2 Timothy 1:10

**Acclamation:** (Keyboard/SATB) NO. IV

(M.M. ♩ = c. 116)

Capo 5: G       Am    F        C    Dm7      C/E  Fmaj7    Gsus4      Gsus4
        C        Dm    Bb       F    Gm7      F/A  Bbmaj7   Csus4      Csus4

1.                        2 and onward

Al - le - lu - ia, ___ al - le - lu - ia, ___ al - le - lu - ia.    ia.

**Verse: (Cantor)**

Asus4           F        C        C/F        G    *to Refrain*
Dsus4           Bb       F        F/Bb       C

Our Sav - ior Je - sus Christ de - stroyed ___ death}
{and brought life to light through the Gospel.

# 14th Sunday in Ordinary Time

*July 7*

(M.M. ♩ = c. 124)

**REFRAIN**

Psalm 123:1–2, 2, 3–4

**Verse 1**

*to Refrain*

till he have pit - y _____ on us. _____

D/A     Am/C     Em7/B     Em7/G     A7sus4     A7

**Verse 3**

Have pit - y on us, O LORD, have pit - y on us, _____ for

D     A7/D     G/D     D     Em7/D

we are more than sat - ed _____ with con - tempt; _____ our

A7/D     G/D     D     Em7/D

souls are more than sat - ed _____ with the mock - er - y _____ of the

Dmaj7/F♯     G/B     D/A     G/B

**Note: Response reprinted for convenience.**

**Gospel Acclamation**: cf. Luke 4:18
**Acclamation:** (Keyboard/SATB) NO. IV

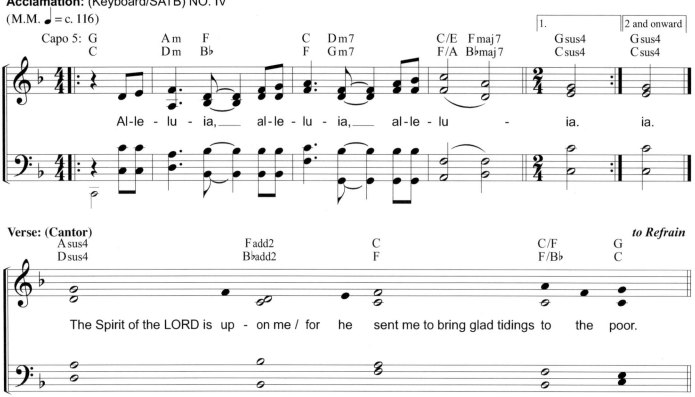

# 15th Sunday in Ordinary Time

*July 14*

Psalm 85:9, 10, 11-12, 13-14

**REFRAIN**

Lord, let us see your kind-ness, and grant us your sal-va-tion.

**Verse 1**

I will hear what God pro-claims; the LORD— for he pro-claims peace. Near in-deed is his sal-va-tion to those who fear him, glo-ry dwell-ing in our land.

*to Refrain*

**Verse 2** (M.M. ♩ = c. 76)

Kind - ness and truth shall meet; jus - tice and peace shall kiss. Truth shall spring out of the

G  D  Am  D  Em  Csus2

*to Refrain*

earth, _____ and jus - tice shall look down from heav - en.

D  G/B  G/D  C/E  Am/C  D

**Verse 3** (M.M. ♩ = c. 76)

The LORD him - self will give his ben - e - fits; our _ land shall yield its

G  D  Am

in - crease. Jus - tice shall walk be - fore him, and pre -

Em  Csus2  D

pare the way of his steps.

**REFRAIN**

Lord, let us see your kind-ness, and grant us your sal - va - tion.

**Note: Response reprinted for convenience.**

**Gospel Acclamation**: Ephesians 1:17-18

**Acclamation:** (Keyboard/SATB) NO. II

(M.M. ♩ = c. 130)

Al - le - lu - ia, al - le - lu - ia, al - le - lu - ia.

**Verse: (Cantor)**                                                              *to Refrain*

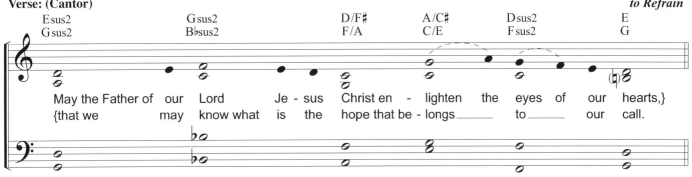

May the Father of our Lord Je - sus Christ en - lighten the eyes of our hearts,}
{that we may know what is the hope that be - longs to our call.

# 16th Sunday in Ordinary Time

*July 21*

Psalm 23:1-3, 3-4, 5, 6

**REFRAIN**

***Complete setting is on page 93***

Complete setting is on page 93

## Gospel Acclamation: John 10:27

**Acclamation:** (Keyboard/SATB) NO. IV

# 17th Sunday in Ordinary Time

*July 28*

Psalm 145:10–11, 15–16, 17–18

**Verse 2**

works.___ The LORD is near to all who call up-

on him,___ to all who call up-on him in truth.___

to Refrain

**REFRAIN**

The hand of the Lord feeds us; he an-swers all our needs. *(Keyboard)*

Note: Response reprinted for convenience.

## Gospel Acclamation: Luke 7:16

**Acclamation:** (Keyboard/SATB) NO. III

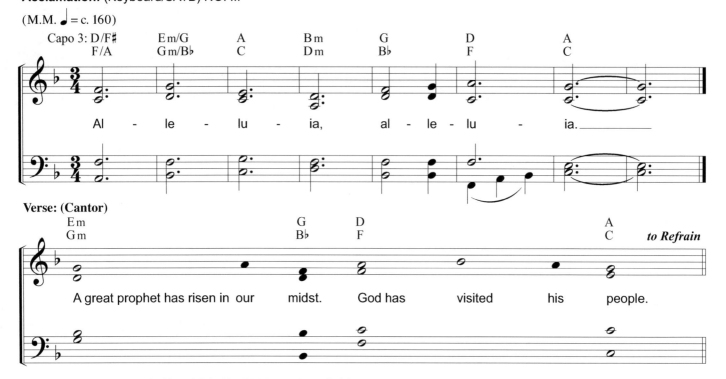

Alleluia, alleluia.

**Verse: (Cantor)**

A great prophet has risen in our midst. God has visited his people.

*to Refrain*

# 18th Sunday in Ordinary Time

*August 4*

**Verse 2**

**Verse 3**

238

**REFRAIN**

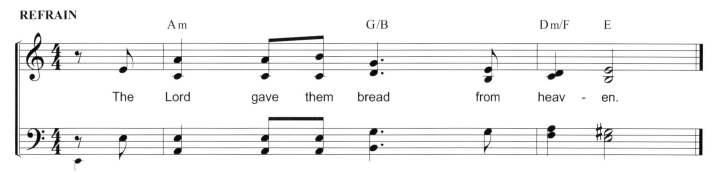

The Lord gave them bread from heav - en.

**Note: Response reprinted for convenience**

## Gospel Acclamation: Matthew 4:4b

**Acclamation:** (Keyboard/SATB) NO. IV

(M.M. ♩ = c. 116)

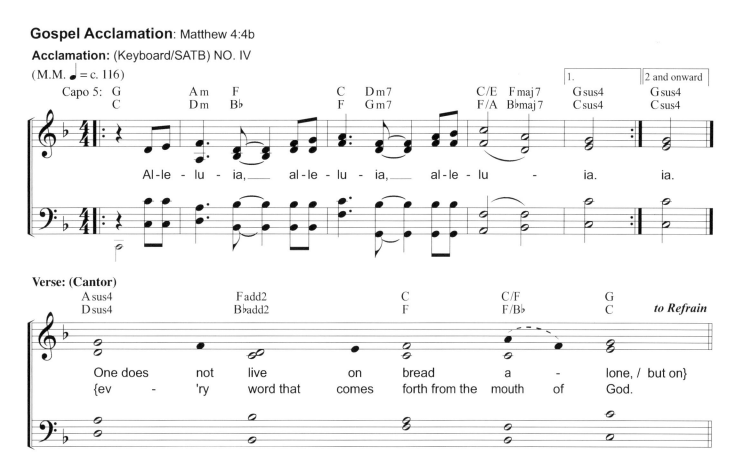

Al-le - lu - ia, ____ al-le-lu - ia, ____ al-le-lu - ia. ia.

**Verse: (Cantor)**

One does not live on bread a - lone, / but on}
{ev - 'ry word that comes forth from the mouth of God.

# 19th Sunday in Ordinary Time

*August 11*

Psalm 34:2-3, 4-5, 6-7, 8-9

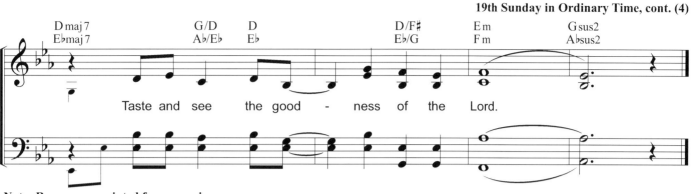

*Taste and see the good - ness of the Lord.*

**Note: Response reprinted for convenience.**

## Gospel Acclamation: John 6:51

**Acclamation:** (Keyboard/SATB) NO. II

(M.M. ♩ = c. 130)

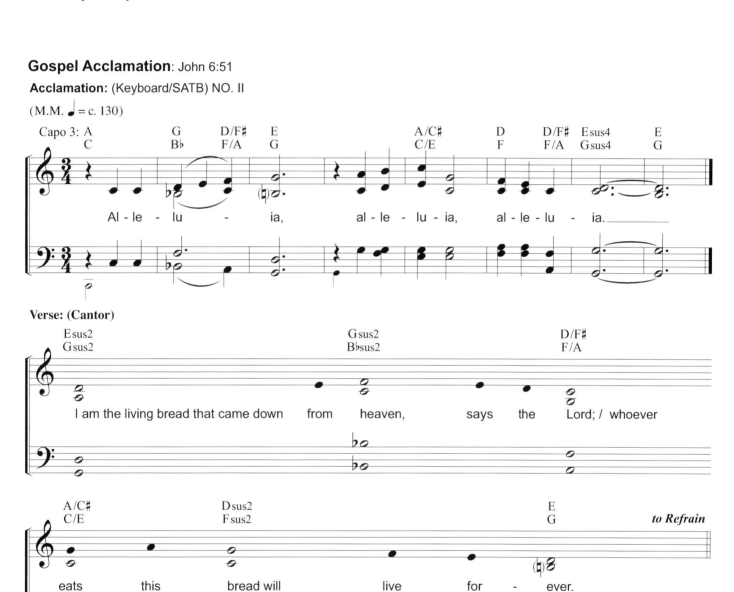

*Al - le - lu - ia, al - le - lu - ia, al - le - lu - ia.*

**Verse: (Cantor)**

*I am the living bread that came down from heaven, says the Lord; / whoever*

*to Refrain*

*eats this bread will live for - ever.*

# The Assumption of the Blessed Virgin Mary:
## At the Vigil Mass

*August 14*

Psalm 132:6-7, 9-10, 13-14

(M.M. ♩ = c. 128)

**REFRAIN**

Lord, go up to the place of your rest, you and the ark of your hol - i - ness.

**Verse 1**

Be - hold, we heard of it ____ in Eph - ra - thah; we found it in the fields of Jaar. Let ____ us en - ter his dwell - ing, let us wor - ship at his foot - stool.

*to Refrain*

**Verse 2**

May your priests be clothed with jus - tice; let your faith - ful ones shout mer - ri - ly for joy. For the sake of Da - vid your ser - vant, re - ject not the plea of your a - noint - ed.

*to Refrain*

**Verse 3**

For the LORD has cho - sen Zi - on; he pre - fers her for his

245

**Note: Response reprinted for convenience**

## Gospel Acclamation: Luke 11:28

**Acclamation:** (Keyboard/SATB) NO. III

(M.M. ♩ = c. 160)

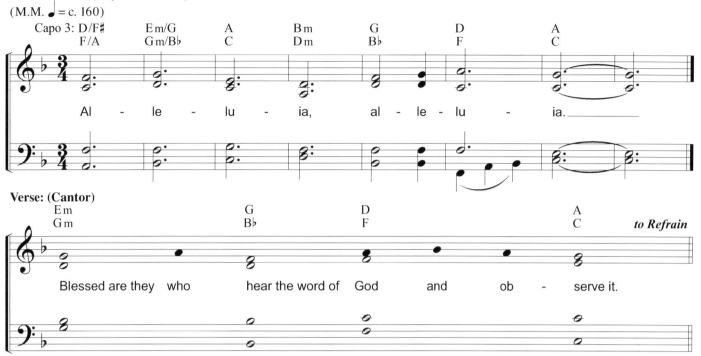

**Verse: (Cantor)**

Blessed are they who hear the word of God and ob - serve it.

# The Assumption of the Blessed Virgin Mary:
## At the Mass during the Day

*August 15*

Psalm 45:10, 11, 12, 16

**Verse 4**

*to Refrain*

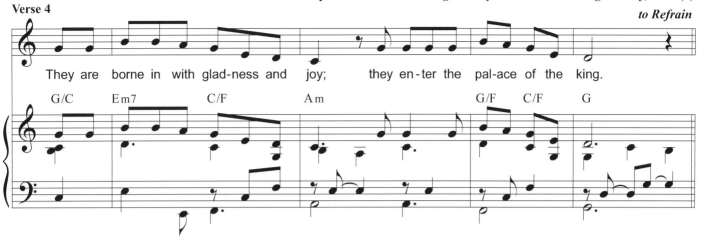

They are borne in with glad-ness and joy; they en-ter the pal-ace of the king.

## Gospel Acclamation:

**Acclamation:** (Keyboard/SATB) NO. III

(M.M. ♩ = c. 160)

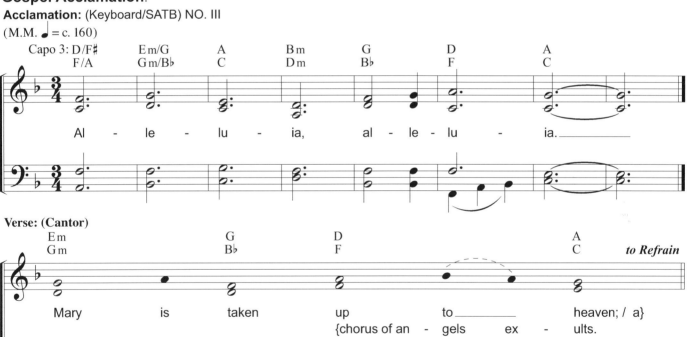

Al - le - lu - ia, al - le - lu - ia.

**Verse:** (Cantor)

*to Refrain*

Mary is taken up to _____ heaven; / a}
{chorus of an - gels ex - ults.

# 20th Sunday in Ordinary Time

*August 18*

Psalm 34:2-3, 4-5, 6-7

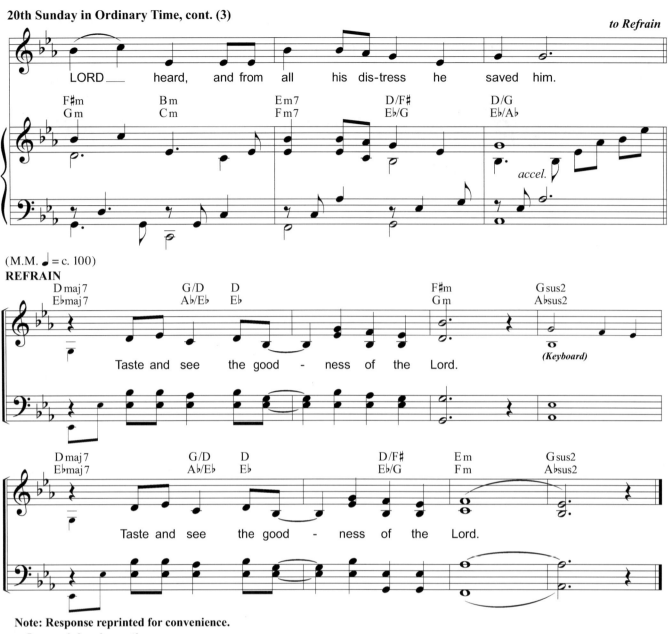

LORD ___ heard, and from all his dis-tress he saved him.

**(M.M. ♩ = c. 100)**

**REFRAIN**

Taste and see the good - ness of the Lord.

*(Keyboard)*

Taste and see the good - ness of the Lord.

**Note: Response reprinted for convenience.**

**Gospel Acclamation**: John 6:56
**Acclamation**: (Keyboard/SATB) NO. II

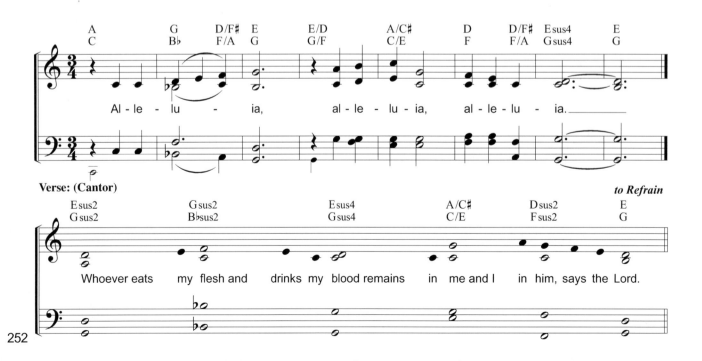

Al - le - lu - ia, al - le - lu - ia, al - le - lu - ia. ___

**Verse: (Cantor)**                                                                      *to Refrain*

Whoever eats my flesh and drinks my blood remains in me and I in him, says the Lord.

# 21st Sunday in Ordinary Time

*August 25*

Psalm 34:2–3, 16–17, 18–19, 20–21

*to Refrain* Verse 2 (M.M. ♩ = c. 79)

low - ly will hear me and be glad. The LORD has

Em7 / Fm7     D/F♯ / E♭/G     D/G / E♭/A♭     D/A / E♭/B♭

eyes for the just, and ears for __ their cry. The LORD con -

A7sus4 / B♭7sus4     D/A / E♭/B♭     A7sus4 / B♭7sus4     D/A / E♭/B♭

*to Refrain*

fronts the e-vil-do-ers, to de-stroy re-mem-brance of them from the earth.

Gsus2 / A♭sus2     F♯m / Gm     Bm / Cm     Em7 / Fm7     D/F♯ / E♭/G     D/G / E♭/A♭

Verse 3 (M.M. ♩ = c. 79)

When the just __ cry __ out, the LORD hears them, and from

D/A / E♭/B♭     A7sus4 / B♭7sus4     D/A / E♭/B♭

**Gospel Acclamation**: John 6:63c, 68c
Acclamation: (Keyboard/SATB) NO. III

**Verse: (Cantor)**

Your words, Lord, are Spir - it and life;}
{you have the words of ever - last - ing life.

# 22nd Sunday in Ordinary Time

*September 1*

Psalm 15:2–3, 3–4, 4–5

*to Refrain*

**Verse 3**

**REFRAIN**

The one who does jus-tice will live in the pres-ence of the Lord.

**Note: Response reprinted for convenience**

## Gospel Acclamation: James 1:18

**Acclamation:** (Keyboard/SATB) NO. I

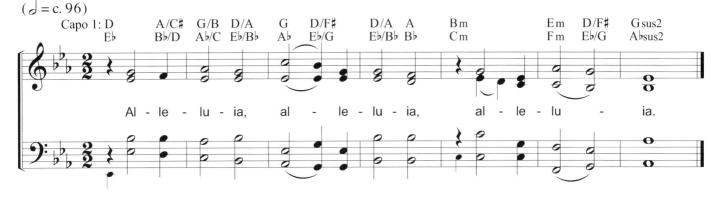

Al - le - lu - ia, al - le - lu - ia, al - le - lu - ia.

**Verse: (Cantor)**

The Father willed to give us birth by the word of truth / that}
{we may be a kind of firstfruits of his creatures.

# 23rd Sunday in Ordinary Time

*September 8*

Psalm 146:6-7, 8-9, 9-10

**Verse 2**

**Verse 3**

*to Refrain*

Note: Response reprinted for convenience.

## Gospel Acclamation: cf. Matthew 4:23

**Acclamation:** (Keyboard/SATB) NO. I

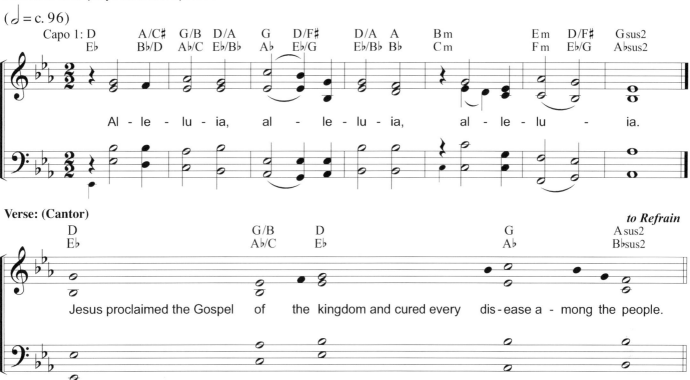

**Verse: (Cantor)**

*to Refrain*

Jesus proclaimed the Gospel of the kingdom and cured every dis-ease a - mong the people.

# 24th Sunday in Ordinary Time

*September 15*

Psalm 116:1–2, 3–4, 5–6, 8–9

*poco rit.*

on me; I fell in - to dis - tress and sor - row, __ and I

Bm7    Csus2    G/B    Gm6/B♭

*poco rit.*

*a tempo*                                                                    **to Refrain**

called up - on the name of the LORD, "O LORD, save my life!"

A    C/G    Fmaj7    Esus4

*a tempo*

**Verse 3**

Gra - cious is the LORD and just; yes, our God is __ mer - ci - ful. The

Asus2    Em7  G/B    A    C/G    Bm7

*poco rit.*                    *a tempo*                                    **to Refrain**

LORD keeps the lit - tle ones; I was brought low, and he __ saved me. __

C  G/B  Gm/B♭    A    C/G    Fmaj7    Esus4

*poco rit.*    *a tempo*

**Verse 4**

**REFRAIN**

**Note: Response reprinted for convenience.**

**Gospel Acclamation**: Galatians 6:14

**Acclamation:** (Keyboard/SATB) NO. II

(M.M. ♩ = c. 130)

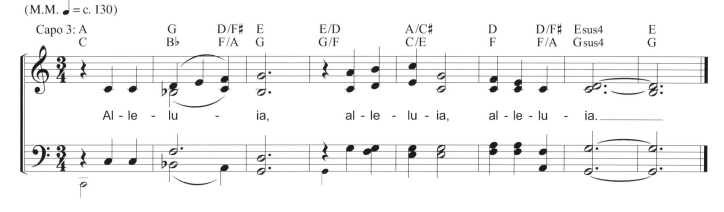

Al - le - lu - ia, al - le - lu - ia, al - le - lu - ia.

**Verse: (Cantor)**

*to Refrain*

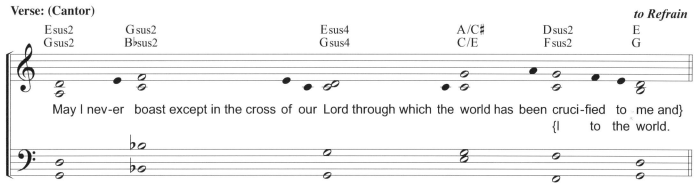

May I nev-er boast except in the cross of our Lord through which the world has been cruci-fied to me and}
{I to the world.

# 25th Sunday in Ordinary Time

*September 22*

Psalm 54:3–4, 5, 6 & 8

**REFRAIN**

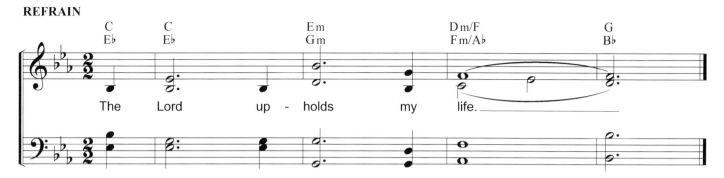

The Lord up-holds my life.____

**Note: Response reprinted for convenience**

## Gospel Acclamation: cf. 2 Thessalonians 2:14
**Acclamation:** (Keyboard/SATB) NO. IV
(M.M. ♩ = c. 116)

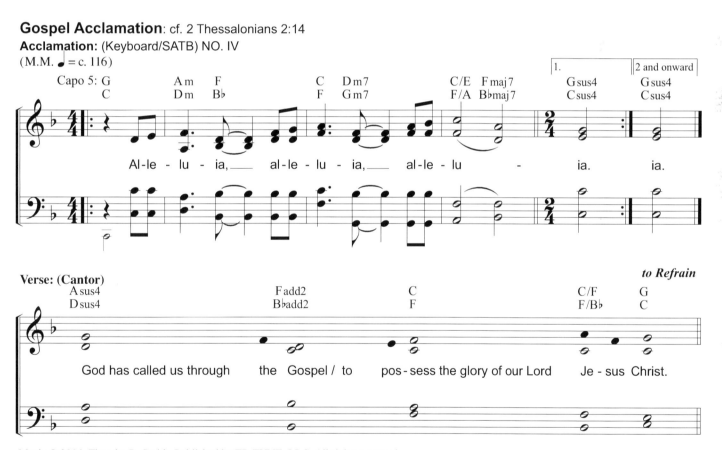

Al-le-lu-ia,____ al-le-lu-ia,____ al-le-lu - ia. ia.

*to Refrain*

**Verse: (Cantor)**

God has called us through the Gospel / to pos-sess the glory of our Lord Je-sus Christ.

# 26th Sunday in Ordinary Time

*September 29*

Psalm 19:8, 10, 12-13, 14

(M.M. ♩ = c. 74)

**REFRAIN**

The pre-cepts of the Lord give joy to the heart, joy to the heart.

**Verse 1**

The law of the LORD is per-fect, re-fresh-ing the soul; the de-cree of the LORD is trust-wor-thy, giv-ing wis-dom to the sim-ple.

*to Refrain*

**Verse 2**

The fear of the LORD is pure, en-dur-ing for-ev-er; ___ the or-di-nanc-es of the LORD are true, all ___ of them just.

**Verse 3**

Though your ser-vant is care-ful of them, ver-y dil-i-gent in

*to Refrain*

*to Refrain*

**Verse 4**

*to Refrain*

**REFRAIN**

The pre-cepts of the Lord give joy to the heart, joy to the heart._____

**Note: Response reprinted for convenience**

**26th Sunday in Ordinary Time, cont. (5)**

## Gospel Acclamation: cf. John 17:17b, 17a
**Acclamation:** (Keyboard/SATB) NO. I

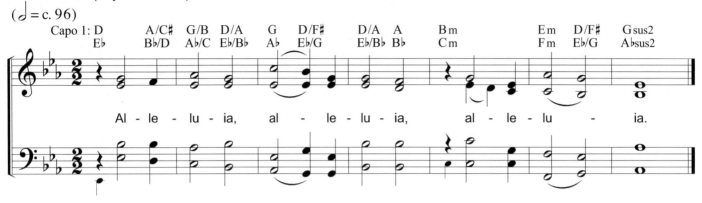

**Verse: (Cantor)**

*to Refrain*

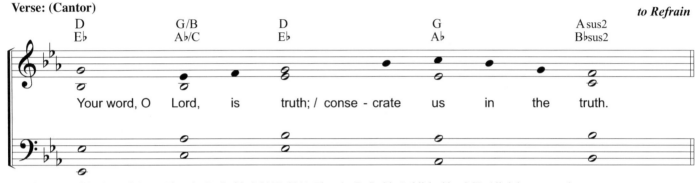

# 27th Sunday in Ordinary Time

*October 6*

Psalm 128:1-2, 3, 4-5, 6

**Verse 2** (M.M. ♩ = c. 68)

Your wife shall be like a fruit - ful vine in the re - cess - es of your

home; your chil-dren like ol - ive plants a - round your ta - ble.

*to Refrain*

**Verse 3** (M.M. ♩ = c. 68)

Be - hold, thus is the man bless-ed who fears the LORD. The LORD

bless you from Zi - on: may you see the pros - per - i - ty

**Verse 4**  (M.M. ♩ = c. 68)

**REFRAIN**

**Note: Response reprinted for convenience**

**27th Sunday in Ordinary Time, cont. (4)**

**Gospel Acclamation**: 1 John 4:12
**Acclamation:** (Keyboard/SATB) NO. I

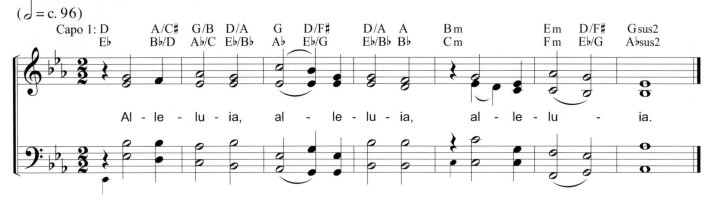

**Verse: (Cantor)**                                                                                 *to Refrain*

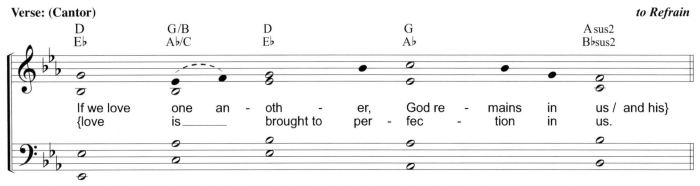

# 28th Sunday in Ordinary Time

*October 13*

(M.M. ♩ = c. 100)

Psalm 90:12–13, 14–15, 16–17

**REFRAIN**

Fill us with your love, O Lord, and we will sing for joy!

**Verse 1**

Teach us to num-ber our days a-right, that we may gain wis-dom of heart. Re-turn, O LORD! How long? Have pit-y on your ser-vants!

*to Refrain*

**Verse 2**

Fill us at day-break with your kind-ness, that we may

hands for us! Pros-per the work of our hands!_____

**REFRAIN**

Fill us with your love, O Lord, and we will sing for joy!

**Note: Response reprinted for convenience**

## Gospel Acclamation: Matthew 5:3
**Acclamation:** (Keyboard/SATB) NO. III

(M.M. ♩ = c. 160)

Al - le - lu - ia, al - le - lu - ia._____

**Verse: (Cantor)**

*to Refrain*

Blessed are the poor in spirit, / for theirs is the king - dom of heaven.

# 29th Sunday in Ordinary Time

*October 20*

Psalm 33:4–5, 18–19, 20, 22

www.timothyrsmith.com

**Verse 2**

See, the eyes of the LORD are up - on those who fear him,

D
E

G/D
A/E

D
E

up - on those who hope for his kind - ness, to de - liv - er them from

A 7/D
B 7/E

D
E

F♯m
G♯m

G/B
A/C♯

*to Refrain*

death and pre - serve them in spite of fam - ine.

D/A
E/B

G/B
A/C♯

D
E

A 7/D
B 7/E

D
E

G/D
A/E

**Verse 3**

Our soul ___ waits for the LORD, who is our help and our shield. ___ May your

D
E

G/D
A/E

D
E

A 7/D
B 7/E

D
E

285

*to Refrain*

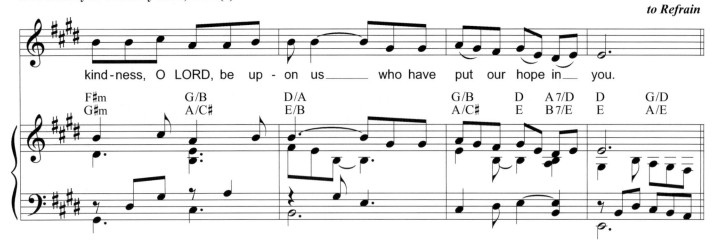

kind-ness, O LORD, be up - on us_____ who have put our hope in__ you.

**REFRAIN**

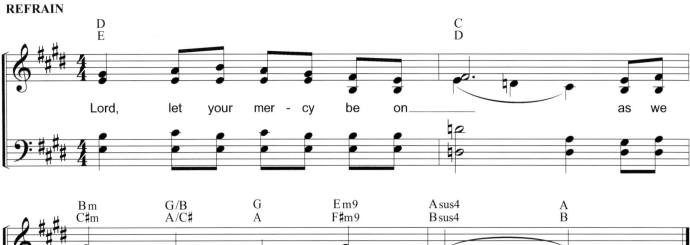

Lord, let your mer - cy be on_____ as we

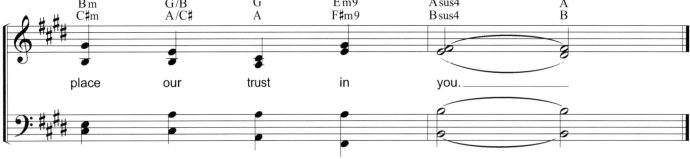

place our trust in you._____

**Note: Response reprinted for convenience**

**Gospel Acclamation**: Mark 10:45

**Acclamation:** (Keyboard/SATB) NO. V

(M.M. ♪ = c. 150)

**Verse: (Cantor)**                                                                                             *to Refrain*

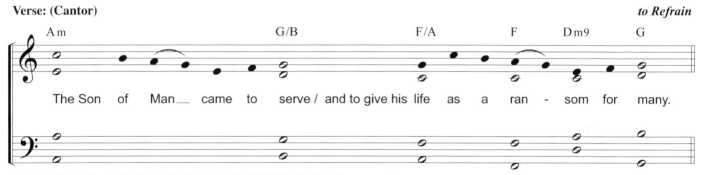

Music © 2014, Timothy R. Smith. Published by TR TUNE, LLC. All rights reserved.

# 30th Sunday in Ordinary Time

*October 27*

**Verse 3**

Re - store our for - tunes, O LORD, like the

tor-rents in ___ the ___ south - ern des - ert. Those that sow ___ in tears

shall reap re - joic - ing. ___

*to Refrain*

**Verse 4**

Al - though they go ___ forth ___ weep - ing,

**Note: Response reprinted for convenience**

**Gospel Acclamation**: cf. 2 Timothy 1:10

**Acclamation:** (Keyboard/SATB) NO. IV

Al-le - lu - ia, al-le-lu - ia, al-le-lu - ia. ia.

**Verse: (Cantor)**

*to Refrain*

Our Savior Je - sus Christ de - stroyed death and brought life to light through the Gospel.

# All Saints

*November 1*

(M.M. ♩ = c. 94)

Psalm 24:1bc-2, 3-4ab, 5-6

**REFRAIN**

Lord, this is the peo-ple that longs to see your face.

Lord, this is the peo-ple that longs to see your face.

**Verse 1**

The LORD's are the earth and its full-ness; the world and those who dwell in it. For he found-ed it up-on the seas and es -

Through composed octavo Ed. 92304, available at www.ocp.org

**Note: Response reprinted for convenience.**

## Gospel Acclamation: Matthew 11:28

**Acclamation:** (Keyboard/SATB) NO. I

Al - le - lu - ia, al - le - lu - ia, al - le - lu - ia.

**Verse: (Cantor)**                                                                 *to Refrain*

Come to me, all you who labor    and are burdened, / and I will give    you rest, says the Lord.

# 31st Sunday in Ordinary Time

*November 3*

Psalm 18:2-3, 3-4, 47, 51

Through composed version in *Blessed Assurance* songbook Ed. 10747 available at www.ocp.org.

**Verse 2**

My God, my rock of ref - uge, my shield, the horn of my sal - va - tion, my strong - hold! Praised be the LORD, I ex - claim, and I am safe from my en - e - mies.

*to Refrain*

**Verse 3**

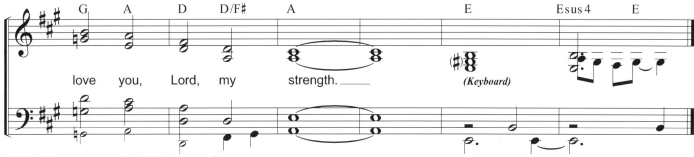

**Note: Response reprinted for convenience**

## Gospel Acclamation: John 14:23

**Acclamation:** (Keyboard/SATB) NO. II

(M.M. ♩ = c. 130)

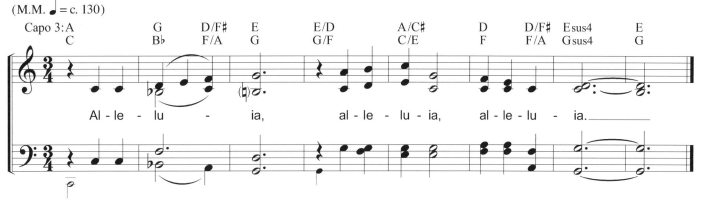

**Verse: (Cantor)**

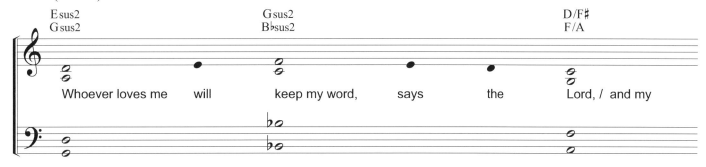

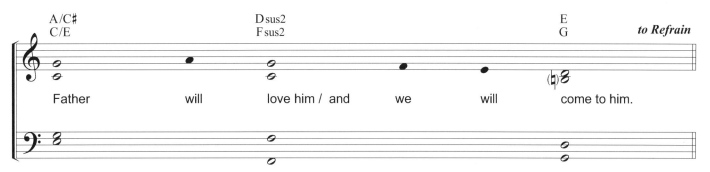

# 32nd Sunday in Ordinary Time

*November 10*

Psalm 146:7, 8-9, 9-10

**Verse 2**

The LORD gives sight to the blind; the LORD rais - es

up those who were bowed down. The LORD___ loves the just;

*to Refrain*

___ the LORD pro - tects___ stran - gers.

303

**Verse 3**

**REFRAIN [or: Alleluia]**

**Note: Refrain reprinted for convenience.**

**Gospel Acclamation**: Matthew 5:3

**Acclamation:** (Keyboard/SATB) NO. III

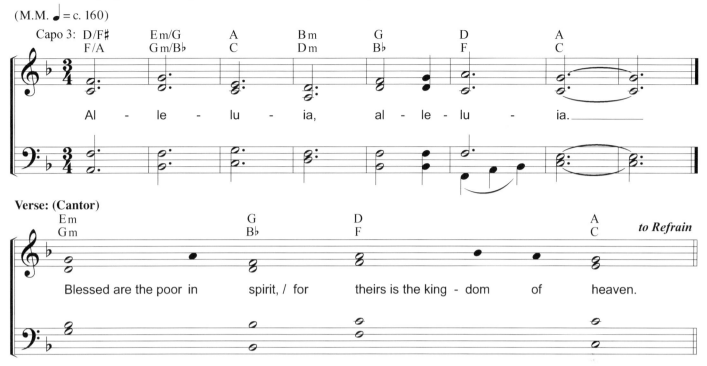

Al - le - lu - ia, al - le - lu - ia.

**Verse: (Cantor)**

*to Refrain*

Blessed are the poor in spirit, / for theirs is the king - dom of heaven.

# 33rd Sunday in Ordinary Time

*November 17*

Psalm 16:5, 8, 9-10, 11

(M.M. ♩ = c. 106)

**REFRAIN**

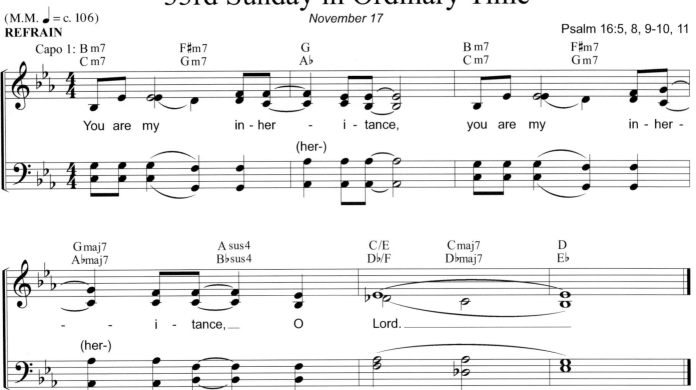

You are my in-her - i - tance, you are my in-her -

- - i - tance, ___ O Lord. ___

*Complete setting is on page 128*

## Gospel Acclamation: Luke 21:36
**Acclamation:** (Keyboard/SATB) NO. I

( ♩ = c. 96)

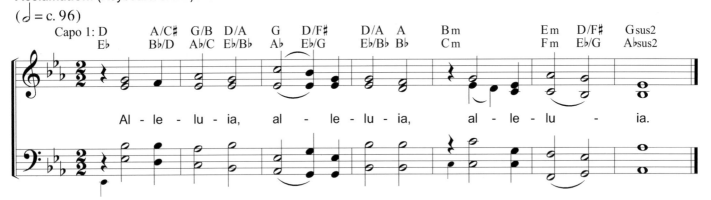

Al - le - lu - ia, al - le - lu - ia, al - le - lu - ia.

**Verse: (Cantor)**

*to Refrain*

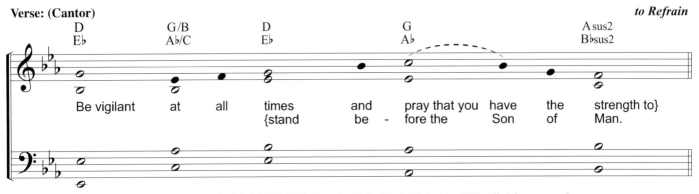

Be vigilant at all times and pray that you have the strength to}
{stand be - fore the Son of Man.

# Our Lord Jesus Christ, King of the Universe

*November 24*

Psalm 93:1, 1-2, 5

**Verse 2**

*to Refrain*

**Verse 3**

*to Refrain*

**REFRAIN**

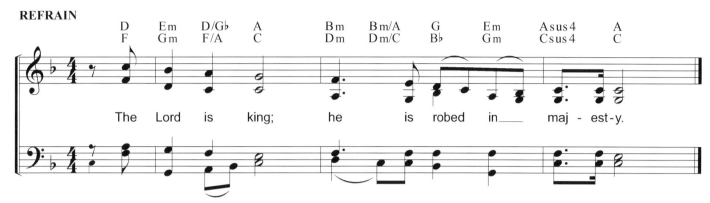

The Lord is king; he is robed in\_\_\_\_ maj-est-y.

**Note: Response reprinted for convenience**

**Gospel Acclamation**: Mark 11:9,10

**Acclamation:** (Keyboard/SATB) NO. V

(M.M. ♪ = c. 150)

Al - le -lu - ia, al-le-lu - ia. Al - le -lu - ia, al - le - lu - ia.

**Verse: (Cantor)**                                                        *to Refrain*

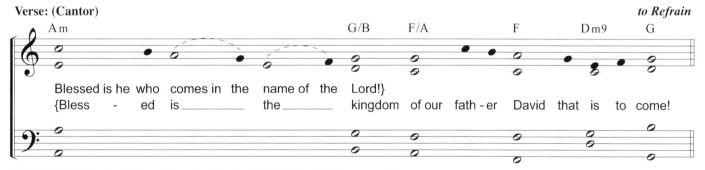

Blessed is he who comes in the name of the Lord!}
{Bless - ed is\_\_\_\_ the\_\_\_\_ kingdom of our fath-er David that is to come!

# Thanksgiving Day

*November 28*

Psalm 113:1-2, 3-4, 5-6, 7-8

For alternate **Responsorial Psalms**, see *Lectionary for the Mass, Second Typical Edition* #945.

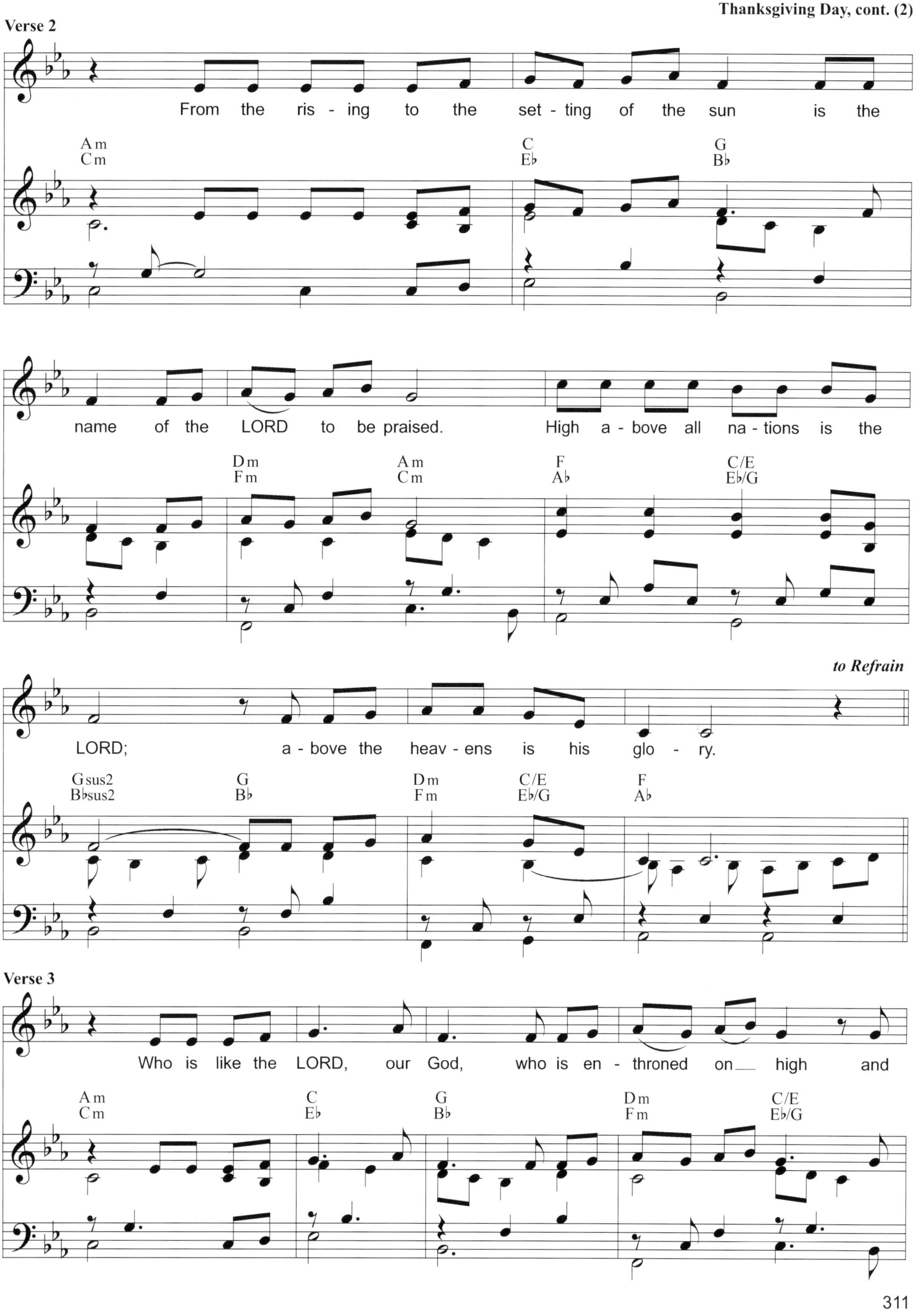

Verse 2
From the ris - ing to the set - ting of the sun is the
Am Cm
C E♭
G B♭
name of the LORD to be praised. High a - bove all na - tions is the
Dm Fm
Am Cm
F A♭
C/E E♭/G
to Refrain
LORD; a - bove the heav - ens is his glo - ry.
Gsus2 B♭sus2
G B♭
Dm Fm
C/E E♭/G
F A♭
Verse 3
Who is like the LORD, our God, who is en - throned on high and
Am Cm
C E♭
G B♭
Dm Fm
C/E E♭/G

*to Refrain*

looks up-on the heav-ens___ and the earth be - low?

F       C/E       Gsus2       G       Dm       C/E       F
A♭       E♭/G       B♭sus2       B♭       Fm       E♭/G       A♭

**Verse 4**

He rais - es up the low - ly from the dust; from the dung - hill___ he

A m       C       G
C m       E♭       B♭

lifts___ up the poor, to seat them with princ - es, with the

D m       A m       F       C/E       Gsus2       G
F m       C m       A♭       E♭/G       B♭sus2       B♭

*to Refrain*

princ - es of his own peo - ple.

D m       C/E       F
F m       E♭/G       A♭

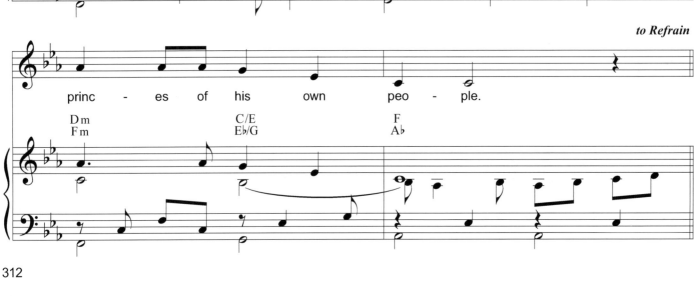

**REFRAIN [or: Alleluia]**

**Note: Response reprinted for convenience**

**Gospel Acclamation**: 1 Thessalonians 5:18

**Acclamation:** (Keyboard/SATB) NO. II

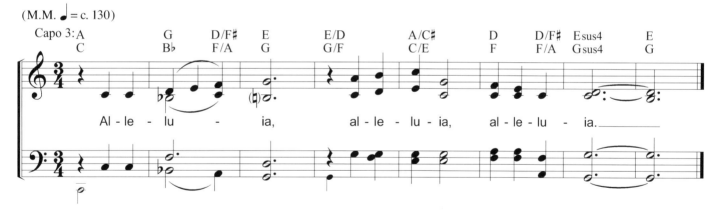

**Verse: (Cantor)**                                                                                *to Refrain*

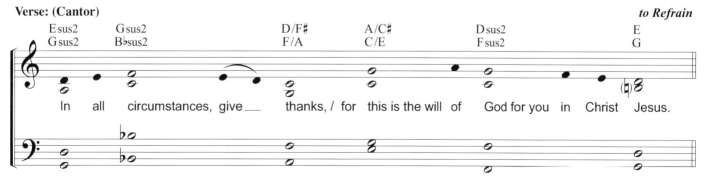

For alternate **Gospel Acclamation Verses**, see *Lectionary for the Mass, Second Typical Edition* #946.

# Rite of Entrance into the Order of Catechumens

Psalm 33:4-5, 12-13, 18-19, 20 & 22

(M.M. ♪ = c. 132)

**REFRAIN**

Alternate ending

Bless-ed the peo-ple the Lord has chos-en, the Lord has chos-en to be his own.

own.

Optional Interlude before Verse 3 & after final Refrain

**Verse 1**

For up-right___ is the word of the LORD, and all his works are trust-wor-thy.___

**Alternate response: "Lord, let your mercy be on us, as we place our trust in you."**

*to Refrain*

He loves jus-tice and right; of the kind-ness of the LORD the earth is full.

**Verse 2**

Bless-ed the na-tion whose God is the LORD, the peo-ple he has

cho-sen for his own in-her-it-ance. From heav-en the LORD looks

*to Refrain*

down;_____ he sees_____ all_____ man-kind.

**Verse 3**

*to Refrain*

**Verse 4**

*to Refrain*

kind-ness, O LORD, be up-on us_____ who have put__ our hope in__ you.

**REFRAIN**

Alternate ending

Bless-ed the peo-ple the Lord has chos-en, the Lord has chos-en to be his own.

Optional Interlude before Verse 3 & after final Refrain

own.

**Note: Response reprinted for convenience**

## Gospel Acclamation: John 1:41, 17b

**Acclamation:** (Keyboard/SATB) NO. V

(M.M. ♪ = c. 150)

Al - le-lu - ia, al-le-lu - ia. Al - le-lu - ia, al - le - lu - ia.

*to Refrain*

We have found the Mes - si - ah: Je - sus Christ, through whom came truth and grace.

# Selected Psalm for Weddings

(M.M. ♪ = c. 138)

**Alternate Response:** "See how the Lord blesses those who fear him."

For alternate **Responsorial Psalms** for weddings, see *Lectionary for the Mass, Second Typical Edition* #803.

Verse 2

Your wife shall be like a fruit-ful vine in the re-cess-es of your home; your chil-dren like ol-ive plants a-round your ta-ble.

Verse 3

Be-hold, thus is the man bless-ed who fears the LORD. The LORD bless you from Zi-on: may you see the pros-per-i-ty

*to Refrain*

**Note: Response reprinted for convenience**

# Selected Psalm for Funerals

Psalm 103:8 & 10, 13-14, 15-16, 17-18

**Alternate response:** "The salvation of the just comes from the Lord."

For alternate **Responsorial Psalms** for funerals, see *Lectionary for the Mass, Second Typical Edition* #1013.

**Verse 2**

*to Refrain*

**Verse 4**

*to Refrain*

**REFRAIN**

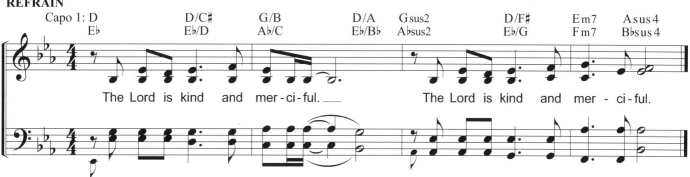

**Note: Response reprinted for convenience**

# Selected Common (Seasonal) Psalm for Ordinary Time

(M.M. ♩ = c. 72)

Psalm 27:1, 4, 13-14

**REFRAIN**

**Verse 1**

*to Refrain*

**Verse 2**

One thing I ask of the LORD; this I seek: to dwell in the

house of the LORD all the days of my life. that I may gaze on the

*to Refrain*

love-li-ness of the LORD, and con-tem-plate his tem-ple.

**Verse 3**

I be-lieve that I shall see the boun-ty of the LORD in the land of the liv-ing.

**REFRAIN**

Note: Response reprinted for convenience

Made in the USA
Columbia, SC
13 June 2023

17806714R10180